NEWCASTLE/BLOODAXE POETRY SERIES: 7

GEORGE SZIRTES:
FORTINBRAS AT THE FISHHOUSES

NEWCASTLE/BLOODAXE POETRY SERIES

NEWCASTLE/BLOODAXE POETRY LECTURES

In this innovative series of public lectures at Newcastle University, leading contemporary poets speak about the craft and practice of poetry to audiences drawn from both the city and the university. The lectures are then published in book form by Bloodaxe, giving readers everywhere the opportunity to learn what the poets themselves think about their own subject.

NEWCASTLE/BLOODAXE POETRY SERIES: 9

GEORGE SZIRTES

Fortinbras at the Fishhouses

*Responsibility, the Iron Curtain and
the sense of history as knowledge*

NEWCASTLE / BLOODAXE POETRY LECTURES

BLOODAXE BOOKS

ISBN: 978 1 85224 880 2

First published 2010 by
Department of English Literary & Linguistic Studies,
Newcastle University,
Newcastle upon Tyne NE1 7RU,
in association with
Bloodaxe Books Ltd,
Highgreen,
Tarset,
Northumberland NE48 1RP.

www.bloodaxebooks.com
For further information about Bloodaxe titles
please visit our website or write to
the above address for a catalogue.

Supported by
**ARTS COUNCIL
ENGLAND**

Cover design: Neil Astley & Pamela Robertson-Pearce.

Printed in Great Britain by
Bell & Bain Limited, Glasgow, Scotland.

Contents

Cold dark deep and absolutely clear: poetic knowledge as uncertainty

My theme in these three lectures is historical consciousness in poetry, or, if that sounds a little too grandly ambitious, the sense, that plays about some poems, of being informed by more than the personal or the local or the immediate present. I don't mean anything as systematic as having an agenda or programme, and yet the best, most powerful, most worthwhile poems carry, I think, a sense of being in a world that is to a great extent formed by historical and forces, one inhabited by other people, living, dead, and yet to be.

Like any poet talking about such things I am aware – as how could I not be? – of defending some sort of specific corner, though I am not even sure precisely where that corner is, or how I might defend it except by writing poems, as indeed most poets do. In my case the corner has gathered into itself a family history, a national history and the history of a second home, as well as what some would call, a racial history. My parents are there in the corner, as is my brother. I can clearly visualise them as I say this. It is therefore a corner to which I have a sense of obligation, albeit a slightly removed one, since I am perfectly aware that it is one corner among many, not a privileged corner. Also, since it is a corner, I am aware of another obligation, which is to resist it and, possibly, to fight my way out of it. A corner is, after all not the ideal place to be and resistance is, I think, obligatory at all times, perhaps one of the deepest obligations, especially to one's own best loved, most repeated perceptions. A corner is where you are cornered, as much by yourself as by others, by history, and by instinct developed out of history. You cannot afford, as a poet, to let it become a soft corner.

My first lecture is essentially about apprehension, an instinctive apprehension of the way things are, about the kind of history that forms the landscape we inhabit: what I see, if you like, from my corner. My second is about certain positions I have seen others adopt in the course of my earlier development as a poet in the seventies and eighties. My third is about where that leaves us in the post-1989 world, because, in my own mind, certain dates, such as 1944, 1956, 1968, 1979 and 1989 have helped form the kind of personal corner I am fighting for yet am also wanting to fight my way out of, enlisting the help of, among others, Elizabeth Bishop. I have little to say in these lectures about the internal conflicts of English poetry, or indeed English history as such. Not on this occasion. I want to begin by the open sea, looking out at it, and, if possible, end there too.

Elizabeth Bishop's poem 'At the Fishhouses' [1] was published in *The New Yorker* in 1947. We enter it through a moment of exception, an 'although', a sort of 'but'... *Although*, she begins, 'it is a cold evening, down by one of the fishhouses, / an old man sits netting / his net in the gloaming almost invisible, a dark-purple brown'. [2] The light is fading: it is the violet hour at which, as Eliot says in *The Waste Land*: 'the eyes and back / Turn upward from the desk, when the human engine waits / Like a taxi throbbing, waiting'. [3] Others elsewhere are going home, but the old man continues working, his shuttle worn and polished. It is, after all, a place of work, here in Nova Scotia. It smells 'so strong of codfish / it makes one's nose run and one's eyes water'. [4] The smell is overpowering, to a stranger at least. We get used to the smell. One does. The smell is strong since there are five fishhouses there in Nova Scotia. Bishop has counted them, and has noted their 'steeply peaked roofs and narrow, cleated gangplanks as they slant up / to storerooms in the gables'. [5] There would be wheelbarrows proceeding up and down those gangplanks most times. Industrial fishing is communal work.

And here is the silver evidence of all that work. Everything is silver: the sea, the benches, the tubs, the lobster pots, the masts, the wild jagged rocks. Even the old man's vest seems to be sequined with silver. Silver transforms the mundane into a more magical version of the state of affairs. It is somebody's every-day-silver, but, as a stranger, you cannot help noticing how the whole thing is beautiful and transformed. It is painterly and iridescent. Aesthetic. Bishop notices the iridescent coats of mail on the wheelbarrows and, as if stuck on the aptness of this description, repeats it, noting the small iridescent flies crawling on them. Fishermen deal with fish and fish are silver. Everything eventually looks like, and smells, of fish. So you become your work, dancer becomes dance. And this is all very well for a visitor to notice but there are limits to such visitors' observations. There is the danger of intrusiveness, of psychological expropriation. So Bishop turns her eyes up the slope to note an ancient wooden capstan, 'cracked, with two long bleached handles', complete with 'some melancholy stains, like dried blood, where the ironwork has rusted'.[6]

This jolts her back into the distinctly workaday world of practicalities. The old man accepts a Lucky Strike. He was a friend of her grandfather. There is talk of declining shoals, then he gets on with his work, waiting, his silver-sequined vest still iridescent, still, like those herring scales that she, in one of those guarded, unguarded moments had referred to simply as 'beautiful'. And there is his black-bladed knife too, that has scraped 'the principal beauty' from the unnumbered fish.

So we have four parties come together for the occasion. Man, work, nature and the artist. We have the implements of work, we have a single, apparently ageless working man, we have met the nature that is the object of work, which to him must be, for the greater part, economics, and we have met the rational artist who thinks, it must be far too late to be working now, in this cold, in this light.

Now we must move down, where the long ramp leads us, descending into the water, where thin silver tree trunks disappear over grey stones, down and down, into the sea itself.

At this stage some hint about the nature of knowledge hits Bishop hard, so she is forced to exclaim: 'Cold dark deep and absolutely clear, / element bearable to no mortal, / to fish and seals...'[7] 'Just think!' she seems to exclaim. 'Creatures live in that! They are not merely the objects of work. They sport and survive in that unbearable alien element...'

And this is almost too much for her to think of yet, so, possibly as a direct result of that, a comic image occurs to her. She has come here before, evening after evening, and has observed a seal: a seal that was interested in music. Well, yes, we think, an interest in music is behovely and civilised, and there is the seal nodding with polite interest and approval, its head possibly cocked to one side, as the writer addresses it, and possibly entertains it, with the Baptist hymn, 'A Mighty Fortress is Our God'. Baptists do, after all, believe in baptism by total immersion. (I myself was baptised that way in 1970, in what seems more than a lifetime ago.) But this is a joke, you see. It is incongruous. It invites a certain self-ridicule in Bishop. Just look what I find myself doing! What *could* I be thinking of? Still, it is a comfort of sorts, isn't it, to imagine an alien creature in an alien medium somehow echoing our concerns, as it were, rhyming with them? As the Baptist convert, so the grey seal.

Then the joke is over. The sea rears its blank face again: 'Cold dark deep and absolutely clear / the clear gray icy water...'[8]

One last look back at the shore. There stand the firs that are to be Christmas trees. The God of the Christmas trees is, after all, our God, a mighty fortress, a grand stockade, and these trees that have been planted and tended, are tall and dignified, dignified in themselves and dignified by work. A million Christmas trees wait for a million notional Christmases.

But then comes the thought of the sea, one last time, 'the same sea, the same', that is 'indifferently swinging above the stones',[9] icily free of the stones, and, even of the world, above the world. Would you like to dip your hand in? Do you know what would happen?

> If you should dip your hand in,
> your wrist would ache immediately,
> your bones would begin to ache and your hand would burn
> as if the water were a transmutation of fire
> that feeds on stones and burns with a dark gray flame.[10]

It would – and you know this instinctively – mean annihilation. How long were sailors supposed to survive in the freezing South Atlantic at the time of the Falklands War? Minutes. Here is a medical opinion as to what happens in cold water:

First, of course, we shiver. After that, the body responds to cold by shunting blood away from the extremities to focus on warming the heart, lungs and brain. But in water this cold, most people would die in a matter of minutes as their muscles, including the heart, seize up.[11]

Imagine tasting it then.

If you tasted it, it would first taste bitter,
then briny, then surely burn your tongue.[12]

And now comes the payoff, the last six lines. These lines, which are to my mind, some of the best lines in 20th-century English language verse, lines – or so she wrote to Anne Stevenson – that she dreamed and which go like this:

It is like what we imagine knowledge to be:
dark, salt, clear, moving, utterly free,
drawn from the cold hard mouth
of the world, derived from the rocky breasts
forever, flowing and drawn, and since
our knowledge is historical, flowing, and flown.[13]

From tongue to mouth; from imagining your hand in icy water to imagining knowledge. Those rocky breasts, those wild jagged rocks, are of no comfort despite our efforts at turning them into metaphors for maternal, life-sustaining organs. It is not our lives they care for. They have no capacity for caring. We imagine rock as breast, water as knowledge, and knowledge as history. It is easy – and necessary – to imagine.

History is a broad abstraction, but from where she is standing, there is, if nothing else, the history of the firs that are to become Christmas trees, the history of the old man who had known her grandfather, who is now scraping scales from herring and waiting for another temporal event, for the herring boat that is out there and which we do not see, but which is also historical, to come in.

*

In all great poems there is, I think, an image of the poetic act. They are about both their subject and themselves, about both the world of knowledge and history *and* our act of making song out of language, singing our versions of 'A mighty fortress is our God' in full awareness – in the best poems – of the cold dark deep and absolutely clear sea.

Listening to the to and fro motion of the sea, Matthew Arnold thought of another listener, of Sophocles, long ago on the Aegean, and of how 'it brought / Into his mind the turbid ebb and flow / Of human misery'.[14] Arnold was writing about the loss of faith, picturing faith as a sea that was once full and, famously, lying like the folds 'of a bright girdle furl'd'; *girdle* and *furl'd* rhyming themselves into a form of assurance with the waiting *world*, at the end of the stanza,

> But now I only hear
> Its melancholy, long, withdrawing roar,
> Retreating, to the breath
> Of the night-wind, down the vast edges drear
> And naked shingles of the world...[15]

So Dover Beach became for him 'a darkling plain / Swept with confused alarms of struggle and flight'. Can we imagine, faintly comically, Matthew Arnold singing 'A mighty fortress is our God', to a passing school of Dover sole? I doubt it. But Arnold's sea is historical too. Bishop's sea connects her with the old man and her grandfather, Arnold's to Sophocles and medieval Christendom. Both have a peculiarly intense apprehension about the sea.

That is not particularly original in itself. We talk about 'the tides of history' and knowledge as something uncomforting and cold. C.K. Doreski in *Elizabeth Bishop: The Restraints of Language* (OUP, 1993) puts it like this:

> In spite of her wide use of tropes of knowing, including the journey, Bishop only once defines the 'knowledge' of her poems. The final movement of 'At the Fishhouses' risks using the sea, a powerful and ambitious metaphor that postulates knowing as a fluid, expressive, but chaotic, absorptive, and formless process expressed by the modifiers of 'knowledge', 'dark, salt, clear, moving, utterly free'. The line that introduces this closing metaphor asserts that the relationship between knowledge and imagination is definitive: 'It is like what we imagine knowledge to be.' Changed in the third typescript from 'This is what I imagine knowledge to be', [it] asserts the social, rather than the individual, import of this metaphor... The experience

generated by the poem is primarily one of metaphor-awareness as a means of warding off or controlling the abstraction toward which all knowledge tends. Beyond metaphor lies metaphysics, in which, as Melville pointed out, it is easy to drown.[16]

But it isn't exactly metaphysics we are drawn to or drowning in. It is history, or rather history as an awareness of dangerous flux. Knowledge of it – knowledge of anything – involves the alien yet ever-present sense of what is flowing and flown. It is part of our awareness but not our element. It isn't Arnold's either. Those rocky breasts in Bishop may refer to a mother, to the tragic figure of her own mother, in other words to a momentous loss, just as 'the vast edges drear / And naked shingles of the world' in Arnold refer to the momentous loss of certainty. Personal or historical, the mother presents us with rocky breasts.

So there we are, standing on the shore of the cold sea of knowledge, at the vast edges drear of loss. I think we should note that though both sea images imply, as sea images must of necessity do, the sublime, the romantic overwhelming power in which we may lose ourselves, neither is a particularly active sea. They are perfectly ordinary, well-behaved seas. They are not in a fury. It is not we who lose ourselves. They are, rather, the forms, the elements of loss.

*

Hungary, the country where I was born, is landlocked. There is no shore with 'vast edges drear', no sight of seals in an alien element. The sea is not part of the Hungarian bloodstream so to speak: the sea is a literary device conjuring vastnesses. Somewhere, far far away, *túl az óperencián*, beyond the great and ancient sea... the tales begin. For Hungarians water means river, the two major rivers of the country: the Danube and the Theiss, or *Duna* and *Tisza*, as they are called there. The river flows out to the sea, but the sea is elsewhere. The river simply flows through us. It is constantly flowing and flown.

In Sándor Márai's remarkable novel, *The Rebels*, set in the last year of the First World War, he shows us the river flowing with corpses:

13

A good spring moon tends to magnify whatever it illuminates. It would be very hard to give a proper scientific explanation for this. All objects: houses, public squares, whole towns puff themselves up with spring moonlight, swelling and bloating like corpses in the river. The river dragged such corpses through town at a fair lick. The corpses swam naked and traveled great distances down from the mountains, down tiny tributaries that flowed into others greater than themselves in the complex system of connections; they floated rapidly down on the spring flood heading towards their ultimate terminus, the sea. The dead were fast swimmers. Sometimes they kept company, arriving in twos and threes, racing each other through town at night; the river being aware of its obligations to the town, going about its business of transporting the dead at night with the utmost speed. The corpse-swimmers had come a long way and spent the winter hibernating under the frozen river until the melting ice in the spring allowed them to continue down the flood towards the plains. There were many of them and they had been there some time. Their toes and bellies protruded from the water, their heads a few inches under the mirroring surface, the wounds on their bodies, their heads and their chests, growing ever wider. Sometimes they got caught up on the footings of the bridge where millers fished them out the next morning, examining with curiosity the official death certificates enclosed in waterproof tin capsules hung about their necks. There must have been a lot of them because they kept turning up, every week all through spring. If they happened to wind up in town, the editor of the local paper would publish whatever details the millers had managed to glean from the capsules.[17]

The dead are the dead of war. The war hangs over the town where the action takes place, over a group of four school friends waiting to be sent to the trenches. The face of war is twisted into a deadly grimace that drives everyone crazy. The boys play dangerous, ever more feverish, pretend-games that cannot – the reader knows – come to any good, and they do, in the end result in death.

Márai's story takes place in 1918 Hungary, in a town then called, in Hungarian, *Kassa*, but now, in Slovakian, *Kosiçe*. The river referred to in the book is, in Hungarian, *Hernád*, in Slovak, *Hornád*. It flows into the River *Sajo*, which itself is a tributary of the *Theiss* or *Tisza*.

There, as the variant names tell you, it is not only history, not only rivers, but borders themselves that have tended to flow and, often enough, have flown. The town the corpses flow through has not been Hungary since 1919. Well yes, says history, but what is bad for Hungary is good for Slovakia. A mighty fortress is our God? No, not necessarily. Their God seems to be doing better at the moment.

And what of the Danube, Hungary's other great river, the greater in fact? Rivers are history made water. Claudio Magris, in his famous travelogue, *Danube*, tells us that the Danube's sources:

> ...were the object of the investigations, conjectures or information of Herodotus, Sreabo, Xaesar, Pliny, Ptolemy, the Pseudo-Scymnus, Seneca, Mela and Eratothenes. Its sources were imagined or located in the Hercynian Forest, in the land of the Hyperboreans, among the Celts or the Scythians, on Mount Abnoba or in the land of Hesperia, while other hypotheses mention a fork in the river, with one branch flowing into the Adriatic, along with divergent descriptions of Black Sea estuaries...[18]

Magris goes on to posit the Danube as the antithesis of the Rhine, saying:

> Ever since the Song of the Nibelungs the Rhine and the Danube have confronted and challenged each other. The Rhine is Siegfried, symbol of Germanic virtus and purity, the loyalty of the Nibelungs, chivalric heroism, dauntless love of the Germanic soul. The Danube is Pannonia, the kingdom of Attila, the eastern Asiatic tide which at the end of the Song of the Nibelungs overwhelms Germanic virtues...
> ...The Danube is the river along which different peoples meet and mingle and cross-breed... The Danube is German-Magyar-Slavic-Romanic-Jewish Central Europe, polemically opposed to the Germanic Reich; it is a 'hinternational' ecumene, for which in Prague Johannes Urzidil praised it; it is a hinterworld 'behind the nations'.[19]

It may be true that you never step into the same river twice, but over a period, you could argue, one bloated corpse begins to look much like another.

Rivers discharge into the sea. That which once flowed, now simply moves to and fro. The debouching of the river, the leisurely breaking, meandering, dribbling or rushing away, is itself a curious state of mind. A few years ago I was at a conference in Neptun, Romania, near Constanza where the writers were taken on a boat trip in the Danube Delta. The experience of that forms the basis of one of the Black Sea Sonnets in my 2004 book, *Reel*. It's called simply 'Delta'.

Delta

Hour after hour, cruising through high reeds
in the Delta. Phalaropes, egrets, delicate
yellowish necks. Fishermen, cabins, then nothing.
More nothing. More reeds. The odd pocket
of humanity, then floating. Each channel breeds
an identical silence in regulation clothing.
Good to die here perhaps, or simply to dream
in the continuous sun that blisters our skin,
to move into an entropic state, to survive in
our own decay. Idyllic too: the stream
lapping at the boat with its tonnage of words,
the endless black coffee. We are part of the river,
drifting among spirits of pale waterbirds.
One should stay here, if possible, for ever.[20]

No one stays there forever, of course. The Delta is a suspension of life and life does not remain suspended.

*

I sometimes struggle to understand what Bishop meant by saying 'our knowledge is historical' at that precise location. Rivers flow, the sea has tides. There are currents of course, but seas don't flow. And yet, it seems to me, the poem is all the greater for this paradox. Maybe, I reason, she is thinking of all those lives floating down the river of time finally debouching in that icy, intolerable sea. Once they flowed, but now they are done with, flown. There are men out there on a boat, fishing, and it would be odd, I suppose, to apply the metaphor of the river to their lives while knowing they have been spent entirely by, and on, and out of the sea. And I never like to think, nor did she, I suspect, that there is only the moment and metaphysics. I don't think Bishop is primarily a metaphysical poet.

She is, however, a slightly numbed poet, one who is bemused by life and is often taken by surprise. Think of the 'Man-Moth',[21] or of the little miracle of the 'Filling Station'[22] where all the rows of cans seem to be saying ESSO-SO-SO-SO, both generous, almost kindly poems of bemusement, or that moment, somewhat different 'In the Waiting Room',[23] where the young girl has an encounter with time in the pages of the *National Geographic* of February 1918, the last year of the Great War. There she has…

> carefully
> studied the photographs:
> the inside of a volcano,
> black, and full of ashes;
> then it was spilling over
> in rivulets of fire.
> Osa and Martin Johnson
> dressed in riding breeches,
> laced boots, and pith helmets.
> A dead man slung on a pole
> – 'Long Pig,' the caption said.
> Babies with pointed heads
> wound round and round with string;
> black, naked women with necks
> wound round and round with wire
> like the necks of light bulbs.
> Their breasts were horrifying.[24]

'I looked at the cover: the yellow margins, the date' she says, when suddenly, from behind the closed door comes a cry of pain from her Aunt Consuelo in the dentist's chair, and suddenly they are both, as she says, 'falling, falling', while her own eyes are glued to the cover of the magazine:

> I said to myself: three days
> and you'll be seven years old.
> I was saying it to stop
> the sensation of falling off
> the round, turning world.
> into cold, blue-black space.[25]

And there it is again, that cold blue-back space, cold dark deep and absolutely clear. The young Bishop has fallen, in effect, out of time, out of the river, into the sea where the waiting room:

> …was bright
> and too hot. It was sliding
> beneath a big black wave,
> another, and another.[26]

A big black wave. Cold dark deep and absolutely clear. And then, suddenly, it's all fine again.

Well, all right. Let us say it is mortality. Or let's call it, as one of my students once did, a reality attack. A reality attack will do for now, but it is time that has slid into it, flowed into it, holding itself suspended for a second in the dreamlike delta of the waiting room, then gushing forth, rushing out of the surgery, flowing and flown.

*

My subject is not death or annihilation. Bishop's sense of mortality wouldn't interest me unless time had flowed into it, because time is where we live, and time implies a historical consciousness, a knowledge that is, she tells us, historical.

I sometimes think the only poetry that truly sends cold shivers down me, is poetry that is itself a form of cold, a cold that is, paradoxically, compounded of uncounted warmths, of the smell and taste and proximity of human breath, and all that human breath entails. Which is, perhaps, nothing much more than just breathing. Breathing will do. We all breathe.

In this lecture, the first of three, I am thinking of historical consciousness in poetry in the longer term. I don't mean the consciousness of the recent past. I don't even mean a willed public act of consciousness like remembering the Holocaust (though I do mean that too), that is to say remembering a particular momentous catastrophe that is rapidly passing out of direct human memory. I mean something more like memory trace, a kind of conscience, or awareness as conscience; the awareness of that which comprises what is flowing and flown, the water that, as Bishop has it, is a 'transmutation of fire'. It is a kind of inner burning that is as cold as the eye of Yeats's horseman: the formation of a poem cold and passionate as the dawn. It is a lot to ask for, but that is not to say we shouldn't ask for it. Or, if not that, since we cannot always have that, a latent consciousness that we might produce such a thing. A thing that is aware it exists. It is, I think, what I most eagerly listen for in poems.

That ambition, that consciousness, is not a matter of grandiloquence. Grandiloquence does not care for fine particulars.

Historical consciousness revels in them and cares for them, as much as it cares for language, for the delight, brio and strange propriety of it.

I want to work towards historical consciousness as something more overt, towards the poetry of Eastern and Central Europe and what it might have meant, or what it still does mean to us, because meanings change too. They too are flowing and flown. I'll edge that way through Joseph Brodsky and, since we are dealing with rivers and waters, chiefly through his 'Lullaby of Cape Cod' [27] and 'Lagoon' [28].

Joseph Brodsky was born in Leningrad, originally known as St Petersburg, then, for ten years, as Petrograd, then, for the next 67 years as Leningrad and, now, as St Petersburg again, though he and his friends generally referred to it as Peter. In his early childhood Brodsky survived the siege of Leningrad, which ended one day short of his fourth birthday, then, after school, held a number of casual jobs while educating himself as a poet.

I was born and grew up, he says in the first section of the title-poem [29] of *A Part of Speech*,

> in the Baltic marshland
> by zinc-gray breakers that always marched on
> in twos. Hence all rhymes, hence that wan flat voice
> that ripples between them like hair still moist,
> if it ripples at all. [30]

and he goes on in the second section to tell us how he was,

> ...raised by the cold that, to warm my palm,
> gathered my fingers around a pen... [31]

'Freezing', he adds, 'I see the red sun that sets / behind oceans, and there is no soul / in sight.' [32]

In 1972 Brodsky was expelled from Brezhnev's Soviet Union and moved to the United States where he took up citizenship five years later.

We talk easily of exile, about how some kind of inner exile may be a necessary condition for poetry. I am not always sure how to understand that. I personally am not, technically speaking, an exile since I was only a child when we left Hungary. Nor were my parents exiles in 1956 because no one actually made them leave. 'The Exile Brooding on his Distant Homeland' is not a caption that would happily fit under a photograph of any of us. Brodsky, however, was precisely that. A Jew, a Russian poet and an English essayist, as he described himself on his arrival in Stockholm, he was both an inner and an outer exile.

His 'Lullaby of Cape Cod',[33] wonderfully translated by Anthony Hecht, begins with '...the eastern tip of the Empire' diving into night. Which Empire is that? It is the American empire, which later in the poem, is equated with the Soviet one ('I have switched Empires,' he says). He observes some classic pediments, and hears a patrol car's radio playing Ray Charles. But then a strange figure, almost what you might call a protagonist, appears...

> Crawling to a vacant beach from the vast wet
> of ocean, a crab digs into sand laced with sea lather
> and sleeps...[34]

Well no, not perhaps the protagonist, that is to be the cod of the title. Nevertheless it is something that might perhaps have met 'a pair of ragged claws / Scuttling across the floor of silent seas',[35] both images of the alienated amphibian experience, more crustacean than amphibian in fact, since crabs are not amphibians. Nevertheless, they have a life in and out of the water.

'It's strange to think of surviving,' says Brodsky, 'but that's what happened.'[36] And a little later:

> I passed the green janissaries,
> my testes sensing their poleaxe's sinister cold,
> as when one wades into water.[37]

'Lullaby of Cape Cod' is a poem about loneliness and departure. It is cut off, hallucinatory, thinking furiously via images into abstract states, scraping the ocean floor of ideas, seeking parallels, personifications ('a bullet that Nature has zeroed in on itself', he says in section iv) and continually talking to itself. It feels itself to be of no substance:

> If you step sideways off the pier's
> edge, you'll continue to fall toward those tides
> for a long long time, your hands stiff at your sides,
> but you will make no splash...[38]

So ends the third section of the poem. The sixth tells us:

> I write from an Empire whose enormous flanks
> extend beneath the sea. Having sampled two
> oceans as well as continents, I feel that I know
> what the globe itself must feel: there's nowhere to go.
> Elsewhere is nothing more than a far-flung stew
> of stars, burning away...[39]

The eighth expands on this:

> ...man survives like a fish,
> stranded, beached, but intent
> on adapting itself to some deep cellular wish,
> wriggling toward bushes...[40]

modulating, importantly, three verses on, to the soft song of the cod, who sings:

> 'Time is far greater than space. Space is a thing.
> Whereas time is, in essence, the thought, the conscious dream
> of a thing. And life itself is a variety
> of time. The carp and the bream
> are its clots and distillates. As are even more stark
> and elemental things, including the sea
> wave and the firmament of the dry land.
> Including death, that punctuation mark...'[41]

It is the cod's song from then on, as it has been throughout. So the poem moves through the apparatus of the hotel room, contemplating the coast and the ocean, with its queer vertiginous thought of Nothingness, until at the very end there is just the dream and the comic, haunting final appearance of the cod as it stands at the door.

The writer is a cold fish by a cold sea wanting to write a poem as cold and as passionate as the dawn. The Empires balance out. He has simply moved from one to the other into a state of solitude that is transient, touching on Nothingness. If, like Bishop, he were to contemplate putting his hand in that water, his wrist would ache immediately. It already aches. Swap Bishop's comical comforting seal for the crab scuttling from ocean to shore and there you have two fascinating doppelgängers.

'Lullaby of Cape Cod' is dated 1975. 'Lagoon',[42] a shorter poem, also translated by Hecht, is dated 1973, just one year after the exile. We are in a hotel again, a Venetian hotel this time, the pension Accademia. The crab here is a nameless lodger, a nobody with a bottle of grappa concealed in his raincoat.[43]

> Blown by night winds, an Adriatic tide
> floods the canals, boats rock from side to side,
>   moored cradles, and the humble bream,
> not ass and oxen, guards the rented bed
> where the window blind above your sleeping head
>   moves to the sea star's guiding beam.
>
> V
> So this is how we cope, putting out the heat
> of grappa with nightstand water, carving the meat
>   of flounder instead of Christmas roast...[44]

Brodsky hears gondolas knocking against their moorings, and goes on:

>   Sound
> cancels itself, hearing and words are drowned,
>   as is that nation where among
> forests of hands the tyrant of the State
> is voted in, its only candidate,
>   and spit goes ice-cold on the tongue.[45]

This Empire is pretty well identifiable, of course. It is the one that exiled him, and he is, understandably, angry. *So*, he continues, contemplating the winged lion of St Mark's...

> So let us place the left paw, sheathing its claws,
> in the crook of the arm of the other one, because
>   this makes a hammer-and-sickle sign
> with which to salute our era and bestow
> a mute up-yours-eve-unto-the-elbow
>   upon the nightmares of our time.[46]

All I have said to this point has been about the sense of history as knowledge. But, here, Brodsky is not talking about the sense of history, he means a quite specific agent of history: Brezhnev's Soviet Union.

How long ago that seems now, how almost crude. At the time of the Cold War, and the seventies were cold, the climate was transitional; now ideological, now pragmatic; now aspiration, now *realpolitik*. 1972 saw the killing of Israeli athletes at the

Munich Olympics. Nixon visited China but the Watergate crisis was just beginning. In 1973, the year Brodsky wrote 'Lagoon', the US pulled out of Vietnam. In 1974 Haile Selassie was deposed, Baryshnikov defected (that's what people did back then). Pol Pot comes to power in 1975, Steve Biko dies in 1977, John-Paul II is elected Pope in 1978 and Margaret Thatcher is elected the following year. The world as we know it begins. In the meantime we watch the unfolding of the Red Army Faction, of Euro-communism, and the usual crop of South American dictators. In Britain there is the three-day week, the question of who governs, Jim Callaghan telling Jack Jones to get his TUC tanks off his government lawn, and the so-called Winter of Discontent. Crisis? What crisis? asks Jim Callaghan.

I know. I can read a time-line as well as anybody, but I remember much of this, since during the 70s I myself was in my 20s, just married with very young children. Brodsky's nightmare of our time was out there somewhere, the chief nightmare being that of nuclear war. It stood there, like the cod, waiting at the door.

But, beyond the specific threat of this, that or the other, even death itself, was the sense, not just of Joyce's history as a nightmare from which we are trying to awake, but of something Bishop was responding to in Nova Scotia, Arnold on Dover Beach, and Brodsky in Cape Cod. It was, for me, the sense that the cold dark deep and absolutely clear sea was the nature of the whole. It was our condition. Nightmares were not this or that event; *nightmare* was not in fact the right word, because nightmares come and go. Before nightmare there was the sea, cold dark deep and absolutely clear, and knowledge that was historical, but flowing and flown. It was history as condition at the bottom of it: the condition of simply being in history with nothing much more than a seal or a crab or a cod for company, or, at best, someone to stand by your side so that you could watch the naked shingles of the world together.

It was history as condition, not history as agent, I was watching. History as agent – the poetry of historical agency and how we view it – is the subject of my second lecture.

SECOND LECTURE

Life is Elsewhere:
knowing in opposition

Because I don't attempt those modern poems
like lost papyri or Black Mountain Lyrics
stuffed with Court House Records...
...nor am I well-fledged
in the East European Translation Market,
whose bloody fables tickle liberal tongues;
despite this I make my claim to be a poet.

PETER PORTER, *After Martial*, II. LXXXVI

The late Adrian Mitchell famously wrote that 'Most people
ignore most poetry because most poetry ignores most people',[1]
and I suppose you could say that the poems I chiefly talked about
in the first lecture were located in a semi-socialised loneliness.
The Elizabeth Bishop persona in 'At the Fishhouses' has a
conversation with an old fisherman, but essentially she is alone
with the ocean and the seal. Matthew Arnold invites someone
to stand with him on Dover Beach but that is to share his
sense of loneliness, and as for Joseph Brodsky's 'Lullaby of
Cape Cod', that must be a *locus classicus* of exiled isolation,
with only a cod for company. Are these poems ignoring most
people? That depends on whether you think most people have
experiences like this, whether there are times when they are
not mass-people, or community-people, or party-people.

But what Mitchell was talking about, in his own well-inten-
tioned, Blakean-angelic way, was responsibility not sociability.
In an early poem titled 'Involvement'[2] he addresses a question
put by *London Magazine* to the effect, and I quote, including

the exclusive genders: '…are you for the writer in any way as polemicist, or do you believe that his instinct as an artist is ultimately the real test of his integrity?' By way of answer Mitchell offers a brief scene in which a man is being beaten up by two secret policemen when an ENGLISH WRITER passes and hears the man's call for help. The ENGLISH WRITER responds, saying:

> Look, I don't like this any more than you do. But I've got to follow my own instinct as an artist.

To which the man replies (spitting teeth):

> Yes, well that's ultimately the real test of your integrity.

As a result, the beating-up continues and, as Mitchell puts it: 'ENGLISH WRITER pisses off to write a poem about ants.'

Ah yes, I used to think. Who are these secret policemen? Has Mitchell ever seen someone being beaten up by two secret policeman in his stretch of London? And how would he know they were secret policeman?

I though this a touch too angelic. Nor was it, it seemed to me, an isolated case. In a set of poetic notations titled 'Loose Leaf', Mitchell warned Ian Hamilton and Al Alvarez:

> Get your blue hands
> off the hot skin of poetry.[3]

The hot skin of poetry was, I thought, unlikely to be as useful as the hot fists of someone actually coming to the aid of the man being beaten up by two secret policemen.

There was much like this in the 70s and 80s, in the latter years of the Cold War, that I found less angelic but equally unconvincing. Here's another example.

Tom Paulin, in his introduction to the 1986 *Faber Book of Political Verse*,[4] refers to what he calls, Elizabeth Bishop's 'sophisticated quietism',[5] and, in talking about 'the witty, anecdotal formality of Elizabeth Bishop's evocation of Trollope's visit to Washington during the Civil War' adds 'if we also know that Elizabeth Bishop's maternal ancestors were New York State Tories at the time of the American Revolution then we can see that this perfect poem is the work of an ironic conservative patrician'.[6]

'If we also know...then we can see' seemed to me a strange position to adopt. It seemed rather close to the questions asked of potential cadres and enemies in Eastern Europe in the early 50s, questions that were asked of my own mother and father. A perfect mirror image, in fact. To be frank, I still have no idea what my maternal ancestors were back in the 19th century since their names vanished a long time ago into the cold dark deep sea, but Paulin made me think I had better check.

'The conservative,' as Paulin had already observed in the same Introduction, 'obscures political realities by professing an envy of the ignorant and by shuffling responsibility for historical suffering onto those who aim to increase knowledge by challenging received ideas.'[7] That being the case, we must conclude, the nature of Bishop as a poet is to obscure political realities, and to shuffle responsibility for historical suffering on to someone other than herself. Furthermore we must assume that she was foredoomed to fail in these important regards, at least partly, on account of her maternal ancestor.

However, Paulin makes an interesting distinction elsewhere in the Introduction, when talking about Dryden's 'Absalom and Achitophel'. 'Politically,' he says, 'it is a dirty trick, an inspired piece of black propaganda; aesthetically it is a great masterpiece.'[8]

Here we come to the obvious, indeed ancient, difficulty: the weighting of aesthetic value against moral value; the weighting of first rate poetry against vices such as, say, pretence of envy; the shuffling off of responsibility for historical suffering and the obscuring of political realities. Bearing the weight of such charges in mind as regards Bishop, I strongly suspected the aesthetic, according to the Introduction, must come off worse. The poem would be interrogated first, but eventually the interrogator would win out.

'Although the imagination,' says Paulin, 'can be strengthened rather than distorted by ideology, my definition of a political poem does not assume that such poems necessarily make ideological statements.'[9] No, but the implication is that we can, and should, draw the ideology out of the poem, as he does with Bishop, drawing it forth as one might draw a pigeon, that is to say in the culinary sense, by means of an act that the poet Martin

26

Bell describes in his poem about cooking two pigeons, 'Grass, alas' as pulling 'their guts out / Through the arse-hole'.[10]

This is, as I have said, albeit by a deep and, I suspect, unconscious irony, an act not unlike the one that used to be performed by the censors in Stalinist Eastern Europe, who could quarrel for a long time – and with deadly effect – not only as to whether the ideological guts of a poem were or were not as they should be, but whether there was proper provenance of maternal and other ancestors. Under Stalin himself, of course, the distinction between gut and arsehole was practically nil.

'In the Western democracies,' says Paulin, 'it is still possible for many readers, students and teachers of literature to share the view that poems exist in a timeless vacuum or a soundproof museum, and that poets are gifted with an ability to hold themselves above history.'[11] I noted that 'still' and wondered how false western democracies should be presumed to be in harbouring such illusions.

We'll soon put a stop to that, comes the implied warning. That is if western poets do harbour such illusions. If, that is, they have no understanding of the shore with Bishop's fisherman, contemplating the cold, dark, deep and absolutely clear sea before them.

Despite all I have said to this point, I did not, nor do I now, feel hostile to Paulin's introduction in general. 'To consider Pasternak's career is to understand how completely the personal life can be saturated by political reality, for politics is like a rainstorm that catches us all in its wet noise,'[12] Paulin writes, brilliantly in this case, and, to my mind, indisputably truly. As he has already observed: 'the ironic gravity and absence of hope in poets like Zbigniew Herbert, Rózewicz, Holub, remind us that in Eastern Europe the poet has a responsibility both to art and to society, and that this responsibility is single and indivisible'.[13]

But, then again, if the personal life is entirely saturated by political reality, in what sense does that recognition amount to a responsibility. A responsibility to do what? Is it not condition rather than responsibility?

A new kind of quietism emerges in the Introduction, particularly with regard to Rózewicz and Herbert, one that Paulin calls 'supremely unillusioned quietism – the wisest (he says) of passivities – which is usually the product of bitter historical experience and which is temperamentally different from dis-illusion'.[14] This kind of quietism is presumably something different from Elizabeth Bishop's more reprehensible Tory-tinged quietism. There was, it seemed to me, a certain degree of disquiet attached to the discussion of quietism.

There are more distinctions. The poet, says Paulin, following Różewicz, is 'like Aeneas in the underworld. Invisibly, secretly, his epic imagination draws on a mnemonic compulsion to pre-serve the past and the dead',[15] and this contrasts, Paulin continues, with the 'deceived poet' who relies on external influences and an individual or lyric credo. 'Such a poet is woken at dawn like a man being arrested or a prisoner about to be shot.'[16]

One distinction, therefore, is between the true poet and the deceived poet. But then comes another distinction. We are now introduced to the lying poet, the laureate whose work is propa-gandistic in nature, ripe for transmission by the Ministry of Culture, of whom more presently. So we have three kinds of poet.

Tom Paulin ends his introduction to the *Faber Book of Poli-tical Verse* rather beautifully, as follows. 'In confronting a sealed, utterly fixed reality the East European imagination designs a form of anti-poetry or survivor's art. It proffers a basic ration of the Word, like a piece of bread and chocolate in wartime.'[17]

*

By the logic of my first lecture, I should in fact find myself in agreement with much of what Paulin says about art's relationship to history. And indeed I do. It is true, I suppose, that the fribble, insularity, self-importance, sentimentality, sheer commercial noise, of a good deal of the art of what we may, often too glibly and easily, but not entirely without point, describe as western democratic society is the product of something like a bourgeois disengagement from history. Or the rejection of history. Or the negating of it. Or, more likely and more often, simply the not noticing, among all the circuses of life, that history is there at all. It is tempting, in such circumstances, to listen to the sound of one's own heartbeat, to feel it quicken a little and to think that one's quickened heartbeat is the noise of the world; in other words to belong to the second category of poets, the 'deceived poet' of false consciousness, who, at ideologically more rigorous times, might be woken at dawn and shot in the morning. But then it is easy to be deceived, and, to be fair, a certain sympathy may be owing to such poets, since we cannot ourselves know when and how we are deceived, not recognising deception being the core of deception. Best not patronise them too often then, either. It is always possible, God forbid, that we ourselves might be deceived.

The third category, the lying poet, is not a category we tend to consider much, if only because we tend not to have heavy handed, ideologically narrow, potentially fatal, Ministries of Culture that demand lies from us at the point of a gun.

The lying poet, in Paulin and Różewicz's sense, may be represented by the figure of Jaromil in Milan Kundera's novel, *Life is Elsewhere*,[18] whose title is taken from Arthur Rimbaud, via André Breton. What Kundera intends, he tells us in his postscript, is 'a critique of poetry', specifically lyrical poetry.

> Starting with Dante, the poet is also a great figure striding through European history. He is a symbol of national identity (Camões, Goethe, Mickiewicz, Pushkin), he is a spokesman of revolutions (Béranger, Petöfi, Mayakovsky, Lorca), he is the voice of history (Hugo, Breton), he is a mythological being and the subject of a virtually religious cult (Petrarch, Byron, Rimbaud, Rilke), but he is above all the representative of an inviolable value which we are ready to write with a capital letter: Poetry.[19]

It is a strange and somewhat arbitrary list (is Breton really the voice of history, for example?) but Kundera goes on to note the passing of the great figure of the poet from the European stage, adding that: 'Through a kind of satanic irony of history, the last brief European period when the poet still played his great public role was the period of post-1945 communist revolutions in Central Europe.'[20] They were, he notes, full of 'authentic revolutionary psychology and their adherents experienced them with grand pathos, enthusiasm and eschatologic faith in an absolutely new world'.[21]

Some of this is, no doubt, clumsily translated, but the critique is clear. Lyric poets – deemed here to be the lying poets – are not to be trusted.

Jaromil, Kundera's central character is a precocious mummy's boy, a fully self-convinced opportunist who does not hesitate to betray friends and relatives. He is contemptible, and is, like the lyric poet in Różewicz, shot before he reaches 20. All the same, Kundera warns us, we should not assume Jaromil was a bad poet. On the contrary, he says, 'Jaromil is a talented poet, with great imagination and feeling.'[22] Of course, he adds, Jaromil is also a monster. Though no more so than Rimbaud or Lermontov.

For Kundera, the chief *elements* of which Jaromil's lies are compounded are vanity, self-delusion, opportunism and mother-fixation. What Jaromil lies *about* are what Kundera considers to be the true condition of his society. Jaromil is a Party bard blessed by the Ministry of Culture. Jaromil is not doing what, in Paulin's eyes, Zbigniew Herbert was; in other words he lacks 'the ironic gravity and absence of hope in poets like Zbigniew Herbert, Różewicz, Holub' which reminds us, as Paulin says, 'that in Eastern Europe the poet has a responsibility both to art and to society, and that this responsibility is single and indivisible'.[23]

*

There is something about the term 'Eastern Europe' that, in the days before 1989 at any rate, conjured a kind of suspended religious awe. It made things single and indivisible, and oddly enviable. It is this I want to explore now. To begin with I want to draw a little on a paper I gave in Kraków recently, on the hundredth anniversary of the birth of Zbigniew Herbert.

In Herbert's great poem, 'Elegy of Fortinbras', translated by Czesław Miłosz, Fortinbras addresses the prince after his death, all but apologising for the fact that he is a soldier and yet the only person left on stage able to bury the prince, saying:

> You will have a soldier's funeral without having been a soldier
> the only ritual I am acquainted with a little
> There will be no candles no singing only cannon-fuses and bursts
> crepe dragged on the pavement helmets boots artillery horses
> drums drums I know nothing exquisite
> those will be my manoeuvres before I start to rule
> one has to take the city by the neck and shake it a bit...[24]

Just who is Fortinbras and who is Hamlet in any given human relationship or situation is open to debate. Someone has to clear up the mess and solve the stalemate. Someone has to be Fortinbras. 'I am not Prince Hamlet, nor was meant to be,' declared Eliot in 'The Love Song of J. Alfred Prufrock'. Eliot's Prufrock acted like Hamlet but preferred to pretend that he was an attendant lord. It was rather like Hamlet pretending to be Polonius. Because Hamlet is the complex man, the ethereal man, the poet, the man who – Herbert tells us in the poem – has 'crystal notions'. Hamlet is at home in Denmark with his crystal notions, his doubts and his thousand decisions and revisions that a minute will reverse.

Most poets are, inevitably, Hamlet rather than Fortinbras – I suspect poets make terrible Fortinbras figures – but they do sometimes require a Fortinbras to bury them. It may even be that they cannot quite be Hamlet without the shadow of Fortinbras hanging over them, Fortinbras advancing from victory in Poland.[25]

'Elegy for Fortinbras' had first appeared in English in 1961, interestingly, in the political and literary monthly, *Encounter*, which many will remember as part of Cold War cultural politics, that is almost to say, as an ambiguous political player. In other words, the poem appears there before it becomes a cornerstone in the discussion of that Eastern Europe where, 'the poet has a responsibility both to art and to society, and that this responsibility is single and indivisible'.

The paper goes on to examine the development of the Penguin *Modern European Poetry* list from 1963 onwards, the first poet in the series being Yevgeny Yevtushenko, who had just published his poem, 'Babi Yar'.

Yevtushenko is missing from the *Faber Book of Political Verse*, which would have been a strange omission back in 1970 when Alan Bold was editing his *The Penguin Book of Socialist Verse*[26] where Yevtushenko got more space than anyone except Mayakovsky and Neruda, and where Mao Tse-tung's poems got more than Brecht's, Attila József's or, indeed, Zbigniew Herbert's. Bold's good-natured and sweeping introduction makes an interesting comparison with Paulin's in that it is distinctly of an older model in terms of both method and content. Solzhenitsyn, for example, is thought by Bold to be looking for 'the values of socialism after the Stalinist nightmare' [27] which may be thought a hypothesis too far. And you would only have to go a few years further back to wonder whether, if only Stalin had written poems, he might have found a space in a similar anthology next to Mao, or indeed Ho Chi Minh, who is also represented in Bold's book.

It is all very well having hindsight, and it is as well to remember that there isn't a terminal forward position to be looking back from. We stand, as ever, on shifting ground. In the same year as *The Penguin Book of Socialist Verse*, there also appeared the Penguin anthology, *Post-War Polish Poetry*,[28] edited by Czesław Miłosz. Herbert was the best represented poet there, translated by Miłosz throughout.

'If the key to contemporary Polish poetry is the collective experience of the last decades,' wrote Miłosz, 'Herbert is perhaps the most skilful in expressing it and can be called a poet of historical irony.' [29]

It was in the expectation of historical irony that the poems were read and so they passed on. It became understood in the West that poems in totalitarian societies communicated by a kind of between-the-lines code to evade a censor who would be digging out whatever he could see of what had collected between the lines, as well as casting a careful eye on the lines themselves. This was what produced historical irony. It was also understood that this irony was a form of sophistication actually more important, more courageous, more witty, more generally admirable than the more aesthetic and decadent kinds of sophistication we ourselves purveyed. So the poems that appeared in *Encounter*, in *The Observer* and in the *Post-War Polish Poetry* anthology were read as much as political documents as poems, or, appropriate circumstances, circumstances unavailable to British or American poets.[30]

In the introduction to the 1968 Penguin selection from Herbert A. Alvarez wrote:

> But where they *[the best Western poets]* create worlds which are autonomous, internalised, complete in their own heads, Herbert's is continually exposed to the impersonal, external pressures of politics and history.[31]

Herbert's circumstances were unavailable to British or American poets. The best of our poets in Alvarez's words, created worlds 'which are autonomous, internalised, complete in their own heads'. These worlds, to employ Tom Paulin's more critical formulation, are those in which: it was 'still possible for many readers, students and teachers of literature to share the view that poems exist in a timeless vacuum or a soundproof museum, and that poets are gifted with an ability to hold themselves above history'.

The circumstances that seemed to be unavailable were chiefly circumstances of actual physical danger. One might look about in vain for secret policemen beating up people, though one might find real, uniformed policemen doing so, possibly in the case of Blair Peach in Southall in 1979, but there would be no danger in the seeing and reporting of it, certainly not in verse. Pissing off – to use Adrian Mitchell's phrase – to write a poem about Blair Peach would not have constituted a risk. And risk is at the heart of it.

Alvarez's argument is the articulation of a conscious sense of lack in the best Western poetry of the time. It was, I think, a compound lack composed of a series of interrelated lacks. Let me list them.

1. Lack of an audience
2. Lack of confidence
3. Lack of a moral role
4. Lack of a public role
5. Lack of a validating principle, or test of courage
6. Lack of a world in which metaphor might serve as action[32]

The lack of a public and moral role is tied in with the perceived lack of common public risk. What poet and public have in common here is less a common physical and political danger, than a more subtle stake in the world of language, where language is as much a private as a political matter.

By a strange irony in view of Adrian Mitchell's position regarding ants and beatings up, one of the few Hungarian poets included in Alan Bold's anthology is Gábor Garai, with a poem titled 'A man is beaten up'.[33] The man in the poem is being beaten up in a bar, not by secret policemen or any kind of policemen but by other men, because, as the poem, translated by Edwin

Morgan, tells us 'He's probably a gypsy'. The poem goes on:

> A score of other people in the room
> They have nothing to do all this while?
> They chat and smile together, what is it to them? [34]

Garai then runs through a list, 15 lines long, of factors that might be motivating the aggressors, beginning

> Their detachment disguises
>   squalid pub-crawls
>   racist fantasies
>   defoliating embraces
>   genocide volunteers
>   jerrybuilt residences
>   wandering H-bombs
>   curetted foetuses... [35]

and so on, ending:

> like snakes all interlocked
> blood-money and forebodings
>   frozen hard in the ice
>
> What if this ice should once be thawed? [36]

Garai was born in 1929 and published his first book in the significant year of 1956 and the next in 1958. The fact that he was able to publish books at that time shows that he was not associated with the revolution, but was a trusted figure, a member of the Party, serving it in high official positions. He became First Secretary of the Hungarian Writers Union and held that position, briefly as Assistant Secretary for 18 years, during which time he wrote this poem. His last few years were spent miserably in a closed institution where he was committed, so I understand, following bouts of alcoholism.

By the time of the mid-80s he was regarded as a Hungarian Jaromil, an official poet, a Party laureate, ignored and despised. The poem of his I have quoted points out a specific evil, underscores it with various general evils, and points, hopefully, at the end to a general good. The Party, a relatively liberal institution in Hungary by the mid-80s, at least by comparison with its equivalents elsewhere in Eastern Europe, could approve the poem without difficulty. Right from the beginning the Party was keen, indeed insisted on, optimism and the poem offers a certain desired uplift at the end.

Like Jaromil, Garai was not a bad poet, and some of his work is still to be seen here and there, chiefly lyrical and sentimental verses articulated with real skill. Nor could Alan Bold have known much about his standing in Hungary in 1970. And yet the man was, after all, First Secretary of the Writers Union. He was not a poet in the Zbigniew Herbert mould.

It is those who are missing in the Bold anthology, as indeed in the Paulin, that strike one now. Not that Bold and Paulin could necessarily help it because of issues of timing and availability; nevertheless the missing are the missing. Two of the missing Hungarians are Gyula Illyés and György Petri.

Illyés was born to a poor peasant family on the Hungarian Plains in 1902. He was part of the workers' youth movement during the brief Bolshevik government of 1919, was highly active in the Socialist movements of the 1930s and wrote a classic sociological study, *People of the Puszta*,[37] in 1936. He was on the run in 1944 when Hungary was occupied by German troops and when the fascist Arrow Cross Party took power. After 1945 he became a leader of the National Peasant Party but when the Stalinists banned or absorbed the other parties he withdrew from public life. Nevertheless he continued publishing in the 50s when most of the other major poets were silenced. During the revolution in 1956 a long poem of his was circulated in the revolutionary press. The poem was titled, 'A Sentence about Tyranny'.[38] This is how it begins:

Where tyranny exists
that tyranny exists
not only in the barrel of the gun
not only in the cells of a prison

not just in the interrogation block
or the small hours of the clock
the guard's bark and his fists
the tyranny exists

not just in the billowing black fetor
of the closing speech of the prosecutor,
in 'the justified use of force'
the prisoners' dull morse

not merely in the cool postscript
of the expected verdict
there's tyranny
not just in the crisp military

order to 'Stand!' and the numb
instruction 'Fire!', the roll of the drum,
in the last twitch
of the corpse in the ditch...

And so on for another 42 verses. It is a remarkable poem, apparently addressed to tyranny in general – and indeed applicable in general – but making quite specific references to the Hungarian situation in particular. It wasn't, however, written in 1956 but back in 1950, at the worst time of show trials, executions, intense state surveillance, and sudden, secret internment and disappearance into one of Hungary's own gulags. It was a poem written, as they used to say then, for the desk drawer, to be shown only to the most trusted friends, a genuinely dangerous poem, written in danger and constituting clear and present danger. It was, in its own time, an answer to the question posed by the woman to Akhmatova when queuing for the Lubyanka prison. 'Can you describe this?' Yes, replied Akhmatova. She could.

Illyés's circumstances at that stage were not those in which Herbert wrote his poems of historic irony, as Miłosz described them. 'A Sentence on Tyranny' is more head-on, more vulnerable, and was, for five years, utterly hidden. It had no irony because there was no secret communication. Or rather there was only secret communication, but not with a public.

Illyés himself, interestingly, was regarded by some of the other major Hungarian poets, including Ágnes Nemes Nagy, as something of a traitor for not doing anything for silenced poets like herself in the early 50s. He was, they thought, too close to ministers and authorities. Nor was he of great help to poets of her kind after 1956. When certain poets became non-persons, they suggested, he did not stick up for them. He was regarded by some as a version of Jaromil. There seem to have been a great many shades of Jaromil everywhere. After 1956, the poem was suppressed again. I myself was shown 'A Sentence of Tyranny' only in a scrappy *samizdat* version in 1985.

Lack of translations might of course account for any number of exclusions from anthologies. 'A Sentence on Tyranny' first appeared in Vernon Watkins's translation in 1976, that is to say after Alan Bold's anthology. My translation, the one I have used here, was first published in 1995. The fact remains however that Bold used none of the so-called "unofficial" Hungarian poets who might have been available. They were, in effect, invisible.

György Petri is a very different case. Petri was born in Budapest in 1943, read Philosophy and Hungarian Literature at university and, after his first two books appeared in the early 70s, was recognised to be one of the most original younger talents. In 1975 however, the year after the publication of his second book, *Körülírt zuhanás*[39] (Circumscribed Fall), his poems became 'politically unacceptable' and he published his next three books in *samizdat*, remaining in *samizdat* for 13 years, while at the same time being one of the founder members of an unofficial and persecuted body, The Foundation for the Support of the Poor (*A Szegényeket Támogató Alap*, acronym SZETA in Hungarian). He was clearly of the underground opposition. His *samizdat* books were enormously popular. They were cyclostyled and stapled together and quickly bought whenever people could get hold of them.

His poems began to appear in the English press in 1982, first in the *TLS*, then in *The Observer* (1984), then in *Index on Censorship* (1985), and in 1986, in *Encounter*. The *Faber Book of Political Verse* also appears in 1986 so there would not have been much margin for Petri's inclusion in it, but there was some. His first book in English, *Night Song of the Personal Shadow* appeared in 1991, published by Bloodaxe and translated by Clive Wilmer and George Gömöri.

In his introduction to the book Clive Wilmer, introducing Petri as a satirist, wrote:

To a dissident like György Petri, Kádár *[the leader of the Hungarian ruling party since 1956]* – 'this Aegisthus with his trainee barber's face' [as he puts it in a poem] was even more contemptible than the hard-line leaders of the other Communist countries. The Hungarian dictatorship, he says, was 'more sophisticated…more clever'; the control it exerted, therefore, went deeper, so the 'moral state of the people was more dangerously corrupted'.[40]

He also points out that:

> Sexuality is often the glass through which Petri discloses the nature of freedom. The same is true of death.... Through sexuality, in short, Petri stresses the continuity of the public and private spheres...[41]

Petri's great popularity was down partly to those passionate dark sexual jokes of his. In that respect he is, like Herbert, a historical ironist, albeit, as Wilmer insists, of a different generation and of a different type. It was this irony – this complicity – that endeared him to the dissident undercurrent in Hungary. Here, for example, is the figure of Kádár as Aegisthus, in the poem, 'Electra':

> What *they* think is it's the twists and turns of politics
> that keep me ticking; they think it's Mycenae's fate.
> Take my little sister, cute sensitive Chrysothemis –
> to me the poor thing attributes a surfeit of moral passion,
> believing I'm unable to get over
> the issue of our father's twisted death.
> What do I care for that gross geyser of spunk
> who murdered his own daughter! The steps into the bath
> were slippery with soap – and the axe's edge too sharp.
> But that this Aegisthus, with his trainee-barber's face,
> should swagger about and hold sway in this wretched town,
> and that our mother, like a venerably double-chinned old whore,
> should dally with him simpering – everybody pretending
> not to see, not to know anything. Even the Sun
> glitters above, like a lie forged of pure gold,
> the false coin of the gods!
> Well, that's why! That's why! Because of disgust, because it all sticks
>   in my craw,
> revenge has become my dream and my daily bread.
> And this revulsion is stronger than the gods.
> I already see how mould is creeping across Mycenae,
> which is the mould of madness and destruction.[42]

And here is the public and private coming together, by way of sex, in 'Gratitude', both poems in Wilmer and Gömöri's translation:

> The idiotic silence of state holidays
> is no different
> from that of Catholic Sundays.
> People in collective idleness

are even more repellent
than they are when purpose has harnessed them.

Today I will not
in my old ungrateful way
let gratuitous love decay in me.
In the vacuum of streets
what helps me to escape
is the memory of your face and thighs,
your warmth,
the fish-death smell of your groin.

You looked for a bathroom in vain.
The bed was uncomfortable
like a roof ridge.
The mattress smelt of insectide,
the new scent of your body mingling with it.

I woke to a cannonade
(a round number of years ago
something happened). You were still asleep.
Your glasses, your patent leather bag
on the floor, your dress on the window-catch
hung inside out – so practical.

One strap of your black slip
had slithered off.
And a gentle light was wavering
on the downs of your neck, on your collar-bones,
as the cannon went on booming

and on a spring poking through
the armchair's cover
fine dust was trembling.[43]

It is as perfect an example as you could wish of what Tom
Paulin talked of in his introduction regarding Pasternak, when
he said: 'To consider Pasternak's career is to understand how
completely the personal life can be saturated by political reality
…' and so on down to 'wet noise'. And how, 'In confronting a
sealed, utterly fixed reality the East European imagination designs
a form of anti-poetry or survivor's art.' That piece of bread and
chocolate in wartime.

I must admit there were times in the 80s when I thought
British poets might have preferred to live under dictatorships
and tyrannies so that they might have more important things

to write about than, as Adrian Mitchell would have had it, ants. 'Shall we continue in sin,' asked St Paul, 'that grace may abound?' In other words should we do bad things, live in a bad world, so that we may experience and feel the power of good? Grace is, after all, authority. Not that anyone ever said so, not that the attitude to the sin that produced grace, was ever unambiguous, but I thought one could sometimes feel the straining of the leash. I don't suppose we would wish for gulags just so that we might produce a Mandelstam. And despite Vietnam, despite Watergate, despite many dreadful things, it remained hard, in my opinion, to imagine the UK quite as a gulag society, complete with clear and present danger to ourselves.

Hence Tom Paulin's difficulty. Hence our difficulty. And hence perhaps György Petri's answer, which could be our answer too. It is what Tom Paulin called 'wet noise': the rainy nights of Georgia, Birmingham, Newcastle, Budapest, London. The rain tipping down. The sheer noise of it.

Flowing and flown:
in the world of superfluous knowledge

In the mid-80s, when I was making my first return visits to Hungary, I wrote that a poet without a people was like a cork bobbing on the sea, that there were certain aspects of a people's poetry that an outsider, being on the sea, not of it, could not fully comprehend, song being the chief among them, because song was lodged in a pre-conscious part of communal memory in which apparently blank and ordinary underwater life gathers enormous unarticulated emotional force. I said this because in my early attempts at translation I found some work, the most song-like work, all but impossible to translate. It wasn't because I couldn't feel it – I most certainly could – but because the actual vehicle, the means whereby the powerful feeling made itself manifest, seemed so utterly inadequate when rendered into its rough equivalent in English.

Hell is other people, said Sartre, but surely that cannot be so. We are nothing without other people through whom we walk and pass our long or short love's day. If we live in the world, as we assuredly do, they must speak within and through us, through our language as poets. That, at the very core, is what song is, isn't it? It is the dissolving of the one in the whole, the floating of single ME in the great sea of ANON, meaning us.

How frightening though to be dissolved, to drown in that cold dark sea with its freight of drifting corks.

There is something about song that frightens me. It is song's version of community. My mind goes back to the three months I spent in Ireland, at Trinity College Dublin, often at supper or at festivals, often hearing people singing. I quickly became aware there were certain singable songs and certain non-singable songs.

The singable songs were those that amplified and confirmed the community's sense of history, those broad myths the tribe sings to keep itself together. The songs always confirmed rather than questioned the community, of course. They were a form of 'With God on Our Side'. They did not admit much doubt. They never do. They elicit tears and assent. They are beautiful and substantial and Janus faced, one face smiling and hospitable, the other frowning and grimacing. On good occasions you only get the friendly face. On other occasions you get the Horst Wessel Song. But our side never sings the Horst Wessel Song, you might protest. That is a song only *They* sing: that only a *They* can sing.

Granted, no one in Dublin was singing the Horst Wessel song. Any fool could tell that. But there was still an invitation to assent, to swallow whole, to drown in the mutually confirmed, affirmed, firm-muscled sea.

Derek Mahon, in one of his key poems, 'The Last of the Fire Kings' defines a certain ritualistic relationship to history and, by the same token, to community:

> I want to be
> Like the man who descends
> At two milk churns
>
> With a bulging
> String bag and vanishes
> Where the lane turns,
>
> Or the man
> Who drops at night
> From a moving train
>
> And strikes out over the fields
> Where fireflies glow
> Not knowing a word of the language.
>
> Either way, I am
> Through with history –
> Who lives by the sword
>
> Dies by the sword.
> Last of the fire kings, I shall
> Break with tradition and

> Die by my own hand
> Rather than perpetuate
> The barbarous cycle.[1]

We should note this figure dropping from a train. He is carrying a string bag and vanishes by two milk churns. Though he is a ritual king he is more like a tramp heading for oblivion. He realises, as the poem goes on that what is required of him is not to be perfecting his cold dream

> Of a place out of time,
> A palace of porcelain

> Where the frugivorous
> Inheritors recline
> In their rich fabrics
> Far from the sea.

but to join his fire-loving people who are busily:

> Demanding that I inhabit,
> Like them, a world of
> Sirens, bin-lids
> And bricked-up windows –

his task,

> Not to release them
> From the ancient curse
> But to die their creature and be thankful.

The option offered in the poem seems to be the old one between aesthetics and history, between the 'palace of porcelain' and the 'bricked-up windows'. The bricked-up windows of the bombed centre make their claims upon him. 'Rightly perhaps,' he thinks. But that leaves the poet with a moral imperative he may be loath to take. The poet cannot be anybody's creature so he must die by his own hand. He must, as he says, be through with history.

And what does history look like from that other place, on the other side of it? Mahon tells us that in his best known, most celebrated poem, 'A Disused Shed in Co. Wexford',[2] which begins with a nod to Seferis's 'Mythistorema': '*Let them not forget us, the weak souls among the asphodels.*'

'Mythistorema' is a long poem composed of 24 fragments.

As its title implies, it is about the interpenetration of history and myth. The third of the poems (in Keeley and Sherrard's translation) begins:

> I awoke with this marble head in my hands
> Which exhausts my elbows and I do not know where to set it down.
> It was falling into the dream as I was coming out of the dream
> So our lives joined and it will be very difficult to part them.[3]

The soul in the poem seeks to know itself but finds itself lumbered with a marble head that is exhausting to hold and is somewhere between dream and physicality. The passage Mahon quotes is from the very end of the sequence, and since it is only six lines long it is worth quoting in full:

> Here end the works of the sea, the works of love.
> Those who will some day live where we end –
> If the blood should chance to darken in their memory and overflow –
> Let them not forget us, the weak souls among the asphodels,
> Let them turn towards Erebus the heads of the victims:
>
> We who had nothing will teach them peace.[4]

Let them not forget us, indeed. So, in Mahon, we open the door of the shed that once belonged to the expropriated mycologist – we recognise the term *expropriated* from 'expropriating the expropriators' – and there they are, the mushrooms, the lost people of Treblinka and Pompeii, crowding, as the poem says, to a keyhole, to the one star in their firmament, begging us:

> ...in their wordless way,
> To do something, to speak on their behalf
> Or at least not to close the door again.[5]
> [...]
> 'Save us, save us,' they seem to say,
> 'Let the god not abandon us
> Who have come so far in darkness and in pain.
> We too had our lives to live.
> You with your light meter and relaxed itinerary,
> Let not our naive labours have been in vain!'[6]

We open the door and look into the shed, we have our light meter and our relaxed itinerary, and we see them there, the naïve ones who have come so far in darkness and in pain, who also had lives to live. It is not to us they seem to address their plea, but to the god beyond. Could they be asking *us* not to let *their* god abandon them? Or do they mean *us*? That we are, in effect, their gods since we have the power to save them? Surely, we have the power to save them but not to be their god!

It is hard to think of ourselves as gods. And in what sense can we think of their labours as naïve? Sirens, bin-lids, bricked-up windows: do they make a person naïve? Are we, to refer to another of Derek Mahon's fine poems, 'The Snow Party',[7] of the humane Japanese party that crowds to the window to watch the falling snow while 'Elsewhere they are burning / Witches and heretics / In the boiling squares'? Because that is done. It truly is done. And it may be so, that we are of that party. That the burnings are far off while our tea ceremonies are right here. Here we are, in Adrian Mitchell's terms, pissing off to write a poem about snow.

I think these are rightly celebrated poems. And we must remember Mahon was a Belfast boy. The sirens, bin-lids and bricked-up windows were those of his home city. He knew what he was pissing off from.

Mahon, however, began the poem not with Belfast, not with Ireland, but with Seferis, a Greek, who talked about holding a marble bust. Mahon's epigraphs are like this. They include passages from Dante, Rimbaud, Voznesensky, the Bible, Beckett, Camus, Russian proverbs, Woody Allen, Shakespeare, Emily Brontë, Schubert and the 3rd-century Chinese poet Hsiang Ch'u. Mahon has, in addition, prepared translations or versions from the French of Villon, Laforgue, Corbière, De Nerval, Philippe Jaccottet and Guillevic, as well as from poets like Horace, Ovid, Pasternak and Rilke. The titles of several poems make gestures towards internationalism: 'Van Gogh at the Borinage', 'Poem Beginning with a Line by Cavafy', 'The Chinese Restaurant at Portrush', 'Courtyards in Delft', 'Brecht in Svendborg', 'Knut Hamsun in Old Age', 'A Postcard from Berlin', 'Ovid in Tomis'[8] – little wonder that the later *Hudson Letter* presents us with poems like 'The Travel Section' and 'Global Village'.[9]

This almost comical sounding list, reflects an international aesthetics, mostly European, in which there is an appeal to a broader cultural base, a system of what are assumed to be echoes, transformations, internal historical and psychological rhymes. It implies a morality of aesthetics, a moral aesthetics if you like, part of whose function is to provide a sense of proportion where porcelain palaces and bricked up windows (and coupling those two phrases reminds me, inevitably of Budapest) attempt at least to define a working definition of humanity.

But, as Paulin hinted when discussing Dryden, aesthetics and conscience, may be separate, contradictory provinces. What then of conscience, or at least consciousness of that which lies beyond the Snow Party, beyond the light-meter and the relaxed itinerary?

The pooled cultural aesthetic that serves as a kind of conscience has its uses. The term 'European poet' clearly signifies something else beside an Irish, English, French, German, Italian or, indeed, Hungarian poet. It supposes a field of reference beyond the immediate sufferings of the immediate tribe. The poetry of Derek Mahon is constantly establishing contact with that field, claiming access to it. Having access to Seferis, say, does not establish that the suffering or experience of the Greeks and the Irish are similar in any particular respect, but it does assert that the ways of reading and interpreting that experience involves recourse to shared associations and values. As Mahon writes in a poem titled 'Morning Radio'

> But first a brief recital
> Of resonant names –
> Mozart, Schubert, Brahms.[10]

Brendan Kennelly, in his essay on Derek Mahon's 'Humane Perspective' (a phrase taken from Mahon's own poem, 'In Carrowdore Churchyard') regards these resonant names as 'a kind of private army of conscience'.[11]

Maybe that is what they are. Maybe that is what we have at our disposal and not much else. Private armies of conscience: Generals Mozart, Schubert, Brahms, Shakespeare, Cervantes and Dante. Colonels Rimbaud, Beckett and Camus. Captains Brecht, József, and De Nerval. The International Brigade.

Aesthetics may be no more than, as Mahon puts it in another poem, a fart in a biscuit tin: *vento dei venti*, afflatus as a loud stink, but the snow party continues.

*

The Budapest equivalent of Belfast's bombs and bricked-up windows were fallen buildings, bullet-holes and shell marks, several score of cracked stucco angels, a few hundred allegorical figures with missing limbs and heads, a pile of smashed statues and broken glass, all bearing vivid witness to a history of ghettos and transportations, ineffective barricades, burned-out tanks, Molotov cocktails, bodies covered in white powder, executions in quiet courtyards, and bones in unmarked graves. The conflation of the events of two world wars and a failed revolution has produced a contemporary brew that is part historical consciousness, part ironic quietism; part nostalgia, part patriotism; part song and part pure poison. The poison is in the waste and, as William Empson wrote in 'Missing Dates', 'the waste remains and kills'.[12] And goes on killing. The terrible butcheries and barbarities of Serbia, Croatia and Bosnia are evidence of it. The fervid anti-Semitism of Budapest, Sofia and Bucharest are an aspect of it.

The poison remains but the human psyche has a wonderful, life-saving talent for forgetting too when it is not useful to remember. Sometimes forgetting is good. Sometimes it is the only thing to do. One might, occasionally, want to celebrate forgetting too. It might be useful to remember that remembering comprehends an element of forgetting. It is the balance that is so hard to strike.

*

Myth is a form of remembering while forgetting. It is a historical process. Illyés's 'Sentence on Tyranny' and Herbert's 'Elegy of Fortinbras' for instance, both of which I discussed in the last lecture, have undergone a historical and geographical voyage from clear and present danger into the beginnings of the myth where Adrian Mitchell's secret policemen have long been at home. By myth I do not mean a lie of course, or anything specifically untrue, I simply mean history's way of turning from event to account, to enquiry, to overview, to evaluation and revaluation, to imagination, to fiction, to metafiction, to movie, and finally to a universal pattern composed of what used to be known as Chinese Whispers: another way remembering while forgetting. Myth can revert to clear and present danger at the drop of a bloody hat because that is the way myth works. It re-enters the food chain and informs a wholly new passage through another generation's guts.

Back in the late 70s the Hungarian poet Zsuzsa Rakovszky wrote a poem called 'The Harmonic Series'. This poem, like Mahon's 'Disused Shed', carries an epigraph in the form of a mathematical principle. It is unattributed and simply says: 'The harmonic series is divergent.' The poem that follows is voiced for an anonymous state official. It begins like this:

> We forgave him this opinion for a while.
> After all, everyone's different and each
> to his own, et cetera. At most we hope
> that in due course, with the benefit of experience,
> he'd see things differently. Gently but firmly we drew
> his attention to the fact that life, after all,
> was more complex than that. We referred to
> the difficult economic situation, the unfavourable
> weather, and reminded him that such inflexibility
> could come to no good. We tried to appeal to his
> tender feelings. We told him: think of your
> widowed mother – or of ours, at least, our rheumatism,
> our childhood traumas, our hard times and
> difficult upbringing...[13]

As the poem proceeds the pleas of the official become threats, then deeds. The figure addressed is fined money, sentenced to be beheaded, his shopping vouchers are confiscated, his ears are torn off, he is dropped down a well... 'in other words,' the poem continues, 'we used these and other methods of persuasion on him. / Pain failed: for all our good intentions it was like / flogging a dead horse; the / harmonic series continues as it was, divergent.'

The shift from comedy to cruelty and back again is the point. The state speaks nicely but it has powers to hurt and does hurt. It tries to stand nature, or at least the laws of mathematics, on its head but, that being impossible, applies its own comic surgery. Cue more laughter, this time with dead bodies: it is the tried and trusted Eastern European way

In 1991, a year and a half or so after the extraordinary events of 1989 Rakovszky published a book, *Fehér-fekete* (White-Black)[14] in which a poem 'Új élet' ('New Life')[15] appears. The poem is in terza rima and offers a series of snapshots of life suddenly changed, or in the process of change. First we are presented with life as it ever was:

> ...A's lousy TV freaks
> her out, with its constant humming, heads and busts
> of terrorists or commentators with El Greco physiques,
>
> grey skulls aflame in interstellar gusts...

But then we move forward, to an imagined 1994 or so:

> Two, three years, there's no doubt now: unfazed
> by sheer excess, by eighteen kinds of mustard,
> I've found my favourite cereal, appraised
>
> the various brands of bathsalts...

The mind moves through the maze of consumerism, before getting on to other possibilities, other liberties, to being:

> ...why ever not? –
> a leader in the struggle for gay rights or the Popular
>
> Front for the Liberation of Animals, with a pot
> of paint at the ready, and a razor in my hand
> to slash a bourgeois fur...

But 'always there is something' she worries, something beyond the span...

> of time or space, from which their combined rays
> are simply deflected, as from bullet-proof glass...
> some tiny dense trapped particle, something one pays
>
> like an unreturnable deposit, like a compass
> pointing beyond endless dark...

In other words something like Bishop's sea at the Fishhouses: cold, dark, deep and absolute clear. It is not the best of all possible worlds. It is disorientating and not quite the answer once imagined to the threatening official with his tendency to cut off dissident ears.

Returning a year after 1989, I asked one of the surviving major poets, István Vas, how poetry was doing. Very poorly, he said, and when I asked why, he replied, 'When people lack shoes they need poems. Once they have shoes poems are not quite so necessary.' Suddenly there were shoes in plenty. Not to mention those 18 brands of mustard and those countless cereals. It was all very exciting. Vas died at the end of the next year in 1991, shortly after Rakovszky's book came out. Vas's death was preceded by that of a still more important poet, Ágnes Nemes Nagy who died in the August of the same year. With Sándor Weöres and Vas and Nemes Nagy dying within three years of each other, the last great generation of mid-century poets vanished, leaving only Ferenc Juhász who, having been an officially favoured poet long before 1989, was thought by many to have written himself out.

Two younger giants remained. György Petri, whose work I referred to in the previous lecture, died in 2000 at the age of 54, more angry and more bitter than ever, writing in a late poem: 'My favourite toy has been snatched', by 'favourite toy' meaning the old régime. 'I used to navigate history's local route...' says the poem, but, it continues, 'the epoch expired like a monstrous predator...'[16]

Ottó Orbán was a good friend. He was just developing Parkinson's Disease when we first met in the mid-80s. Orbán was the closest thing to a daily chronicler of Hungary's social and political life, writing his unrhymed, loosely hexametric sonnets from what would turn out to be his long deathbed. In 1989 he wrote 'A Roman Considers the Christians':

May the gods forgive me but I really can't abide them.
Their idea is a great one, but look at them all:
a bunch of quarrelsome eggheads picking their noses,
who, under the spell of their thesis, would if they could
be hard-line dictators, all for the sake of tolerance naturally,
who'd not kill with weapons but with murderous disdain,
while breeding their own sloppy aristocracy,
along with other oppressive, life-hating state institutions...
So, let me embellish this with a gesture – a fig for them all!
Just one little problem: the starved lion bawling in the arena...
There are plenty with vision, but they are the ones prepared to be
    eaten,
in dust clouds of water-cannon where out of the screaming and
    bloodshed
something emerges...the same thing? The worse? Or the better?
The gods only know, if they know, what lies in the future...[17]

'Let the god not abandon us...' wrote Mahon. It was not that the groundswell of the new world – Zsuzsa Rakoszky's *New Life* – would necessarily bring about something indubitably worse, it was just that those who were striving hardest to bring it about did not altogether assure Orbán.

By 2002 almost all the major figures of the period 1948–1989 were gone. The world that had formed them had vanished and its going seemed to suck the life from them. There were shoes in plenty, there were many kinds of mustard. Secret policemen were no longer beating up people in the street (the ordinary police were doing that as late as 1988). Poets were free to piss off and write poems about ants, ants that were just ants, not symbols of something else, ants that were mysterious and distinct forms of life.

The ant too was knowledge, historical knowledge, the flowing and flown.

*

Petri's and Orbán's were personal tragedies. Their deaths, following the loss of their toys, or, if we are to appropriate grander language, the very ground of being, seems to support Tom Paulin's hunch that the Eastern European poet's responsibility to society was of a thoroughly soaked through, visceral kind.

Historical scale is hard to grasp. In 1991, the year of Vas and Nemes Nagy's deaths, Oxford University Press published the Romanian poet. Daniela Crasnaru's *Letters from Darkness*,[18] translated by Fleur Adcock. In her Foreword, Adcock says:

> Her poetry has been highly praised by the critics. Like all Romanian poets writing under censorship she adopted the device of shrouding her work heavily in metaphors and imagery, but this did not conceal from her fellow-writers and other discerning readers its subtext of hostility towards state and what was being inflicted on the people. Her books continued to be published, with an increasing number of deletions, but she was regarded with suspicion by the authorities.[19]

This is the classic pattern we know well. It requires a body of discerning readers and a subtext of hostility couched in metaphors and images. As Tom Paulin himself writes in a poem, adopting the voice of the censor: 'This poem about a bear / Is not a poem about a bear.'[20]

51

Adcock goes on:

> During the second half of the 1980's she *[Crasnaru]* wrote, in addition to the 'public' poems, a series of secret ones which she kept hidden in her aunt's cellar, in a box under some onions, because her own flat was likely to be searched.[21]

Adcock adds:

> After the revolution she wrote to me saying: 'Now I am free to send you my real poems.'[22]

Adcock glosses this in a parenthesis, saying: '"Real" in this context means honest or truthful.' But having said this she draws back a moment to qualify it with the remark: 'her earlier work, with its tense subtleties, is nonetheless real as artistic achievement'.[23]

'Real as artistic achievement' is the key phrase. It is hard to say this but, in my opinion, ironically, the secret 'real' poems were nowhere near as good as 'public' coded ones.

Here are two short poems by Crasnaru, the first from the public' or 'unreal' file, the second from the secret 'real' file:

Pastel

It smells of winter –
of rotting wood, of the dark, of tears,
whose rounded ends are little spheres;
a slow current where poisons flow
into what was pure – best not to know;
a life stopped suddenly, in a vein,
a wound opened without pain,
a scream stifled in bales of floss,
a new loss added to loss.
It smells of fear, of plants that will die;
it smells of earth smeared over the sky.[24]

Love Poem in Captivity

They listen to everything.
They spy on everything.
They know everything.

I'm afraid of the furniture, the walls, the cat purring
on the cold radiator.
I'm afraid of friends, of my own child.
I'm afraid of myself.
On the telephone I talk about the weather,
about yesterday's football match.
About nothing.
I'd like to tell you, darling,
that I love you.
But I must be cautious
because who knows what *they* might think I meant by that? [25]

I am aware that I am reading these poems from the Western,
non-Romanian point of view, but it seems to me that the first,
public, poem is far better than the second secret one. Who knows
whether things as they look from the snow party's point of view
bear much relation to the way they look from the burning squares?
We cannot know. All we know is that, as far as Crasnaru is
concerned we are of the snow party; of the snow party, albeit
with a certain obligation not to ignore those burning squares.
Nor should we, we gods, as we might feel, abandon our own
disused sheds: equipped as we are with our light meters and
relaxed itineraries, we should not let their prisoners' naïve
labours be in vain.

*

What of the successors of Petri and Orbán and Crasnaru, of
those whose formative years – if that is what they are – were
spent in the years following 1989? Clearly, their relationship
with society, a society of shoes, mustard and political chaos,
would be different. I say political chaos because what succeeds
1989 is not some new version of the past, not a replay of pre-
communist 1946. There are certain similarities – huge inflation,
collapse of pensions and state benefits, a clamour among various
old and new political parties to seize opportunity and establish
themselves as powers. There is, perhaps a similar sense of crawl-
ing, Anselm Kiefer-like, out from under the rubble. Sometimes
I think Eastern Europe – and I know Hungary best, of course
– has proceeded from disillusion to disillusion without an inter-
vening period of comforting illusion.

We should not think that there were illusions. We should not think of the labours of Eastern Europe as, in Mahon's terms, naïve. To think so would, I think, be our illusion, our naivety. Some time during 1989 a Hungarian editor showed me a letter from one of the better known translators in which the translator, a Canadian, wrote that he was very excited by what was happening in Budapest but that he hoped Budapest would not simply become another Vancouver.

That, to me, seemed strange, improper plea: as if the choice for Budapest was either to be 'itself' or Vancouver. Not that the writer had any intention of coming to live in the old Budapest. No, I thought, he wanted Budapest to perform a particular role in his comfortable imagination. He wanted the myth both ways. He wanted to perpetuate a moral arena in which his own ideological and moral demons might exercise themselves. He wanted it, patronisingly enough, over *there*. He wanted an ideal located in a desirable, distant suburb of the imagination. What Budapest wanted, in so far as he knew, was of no importance.

Budapest, like any capital, is not to be confused with the rest of the country. The capital generally bears its disillusions in its own traditionally humorous bitter-sweet, more or less liberal, most-of-the-time way. After 1989 the old left-right dichotomy failed. Petri and Orbán were both of the left in historical terms, but after 1989 there was no such place to be. The political balance was quickly redefined, as if by default, along cultural lines. The roots of these cultural groupings went back to the last century, to Hungary's late feudal roots. They described atavistic tendencies more than programmes. One group was nationalistic, ruralist, conservative and atavistic, the other internationalist, urban, liberal and cosmopolitan. Neither could be properly described as left or right: both found representation in major new parties. Relations between the two groups, that had been joined in opposition before the fall of the old regime, quickly degenerated to visceral hatred. Writers who had been friends for decades suddenly stopped talking to each other. There were riots on the streets of Budapest last year. By the time I deliver this lecture there will probably have been more this year.

These are products of the left-overs of history. Sometimes it seems that is all there is: the left-overs. The waste. The waste that remains, the waste that remains and kills.

It is this set of confusions and disillusions that the new generation of poets entered as adults. Public politics, party politics, was fast becoming a poisoned terrain. No one with a poet's care for words could survive there. Now that 1989 is 20 years away we can see the 90s as a peculiar period of transition when writers became presidents and ministers. Daniela Crasnaru became a Romanian MP, Grete Tartler, another Romanian poet, became an ambassador. One of my editors in Budapest who spoke Portuguese was dispatched to Brazil as ambassador, another became press secretary in London. A friend, the short-story writer, essayist and translator, Árpád Göncz was president of Hungary for eight years. We are familiar with Havel, of course. The dissident figures of 1989 generally served a term or so in the political sphere before leaving it, exhausted, out-manoeuvred, and disillusioned.

Under the circumstances writing poems that have some kind of finger on some kind of social pulse is rather difficult. One of the younger Hungarian poets, not, I think, regarded as being of the mainstream, is Virág Erdös, who writes mostly prose poems that can go a little like this:

Vision
(Game Over)

'*Woe, woe, woe*' (Rev 8.13)

The first angel is, I think, the Mirage 2000. The extent of its knowledge is enough to bring all heaven crashing about our ears... I am not particularly a thrill seeker but I'd still like to see it. I zip here and there about the sky, cast my eyes round and relax, while under me the bridges break up like pretzels.

The second angel is, I think, His Highness, Wacko Jacko. What I like about him is that he never ages. He's as old as my great-great-grandad but he looks barely twenty. Of course there's a trick involved: music certainly helps. The trick is that he has been distilled into a quasi-essence. Even his colon is pure alchemical gold. When I think about it I can see this is the way the world works. Have fuck all to do with shit of any sort. Get rid of it.

The third angel is, I think, the Doberman bitch. Not the flat-arse kind, but the other one. The most recent breed that comes with replaceable dentures that you can whip out at night, and slip into a little bag...and, should you feel an overwhelming desire to screw her for instance, you can bang away without worrying. She won't bite your neck while you're doing it.

The fourth angel is, I think, an electronic woman. Her advantage is that she has a meter on her back which will tell you exactly how effective your blows are. Of course you can do plenty of other things with her besides hitting her. She costs relatively little to run. You can plug her into the mains and she is completely sterile.

The Fifth Angel is, I think, Testicle Baked in a Roll. In the Admiral Bar apparently they use male apes, but I have a suspicion they add a little something extra. I particularly like them a touch overdone.

The Sixth Angel is, I think, the new Renault Mégane. The gimmick is that it has no brakes. However much people jump up and down there is no need to stop. And it makes no difference if you lose your temper. You can easily wash the blood off the grille.

The Seventh Angel is, I think, is a goddam little yellow zombie. You attack it, thinking to beat it to a pulp, but it slips through your fingers again. **Zero credit** the machine proclaims with finality. It judders, ticks, waits a while longer, then turns off. And then the bastard produces a message that says you have no more lives left.[26]

It has a kind of raunchiness. The attack is broad and vigorous. What it criticises, with considerable feminist venom, is what Zsuzsa Rakovszky talked of in her poem, 'New Life': a feral consumerism whose razor teeth are firmly clamped around the imagination. It is not, however, a party political poem or even an ideological poem. Nor is there any clear and present danger for the poet unless she happens to be beaten up by a drunken mob at a bad place in the city centre. They would not constitute a secret police. In fact it is just as likely that the brutality would register with them: they might actually like the poem.

Technically the new generation is often formal, playing with rhyme and metre. Not one of the generation is likely to have a career in politics or diplomacy. They may belong to political parties, but the language and themes of politics are far from them. Political language as such is compromised. Ideas themselves are compromised. Does that mean that Budapest has become

London? Or Vancouver? Or, for that matter The Maritimes in Nova Scotia?

*

A scream, the echo of a scream, hangs over that Nova Scotian village. No one hears it; it hangs there forever, a slight stain in those pure blue skies, skies that travelers compare to those of Switzerland, too dark, too blue, so that they seem to keep on darkening a little more around the horizon – or is it around the rims of the eyes? – the color of the cloud of bloom on the elm trees, the violet on the fields of oats; something darkening over the woods and waters as well as the sky. The scream hangs like that, unheard, in memory – in the past, in the present, and those years between. It was not even loud to begin with, perhaps. It just came there to live, forever – not loud, just alive forever.

So begins Elizabeth Bishop's story, 'In the Village'.[27] The scream is that of the mother being fitted with a purple dress after almost five years of mourning in black. That is, we might say, a personal story – a key story for Bishop, what Anne Stevenson in her *Between the Iceberg and the Ship*[28] calls 'the pivotal fact of Elizabeth Bishop's lifework'. Here in the 'real-life story' as she calls it, 'the psychic wound, the shadowy pain that in one sense is so often under or between Bishop's lines is made explicit'.[29]

It is certainly a scream in personal space, 'hanging there unheard, in memory',[30] as Bishop puts it, but unless one is going to read writing for the light it throws on the writer, it is not a closed personal space: like any event in literature it simply comes to us by way of our sense of being a person. The death of Bishop's father from Bright's Disease and the subsequent madness of her mother, traumatic as they would have been, were not the product of abstract forces, social or political or economic, not at least in the ways we tend to understand such things: they would have struck the young Bishop as random.

The interesting, I would say remarkable, feature of 'In the Village' is that it actually involves the village, in that we see a great deal of it. The village is introduced to us name by name, location by location. It is itemised much like the mother's belongings.

A white hat. White embroidered parasol. Black shoes with buckles glistening like the dust in the blacksmith's shop. A silver mesh bag. A silver calling-card case on a little chain...[31]

As with the mother's belongings so with the horse in the blacksmith's shop.

Manure piles up behind him, suddenly, neatly. He too is very much at home. He is enormous. His rump is like a brown, glossy globe of the whole brown world. His ears are secret entrances to the underworld. His nose is supposed to feel like velvet and does, with ink spots under milk all over its pink...[32]

Then there is the store:

The store is high, and a faded gray-blue with tall windows built on a long high stoop of gray-blue cement with an iron hitching rail along it. Today, in one window there are big cardboard easels, shaped like houses...[33]

And so on through everything, the people, their houses (we pass Mrs Peppard's house, we pass Mrs McNeil's house, we pass Mrs Geddes's house, we pass Hill's store...) their houses, their soft flat voices so reminiscent of the bus passengers in 'The Moose', their manners, their animals. The personal is not privileged. It is not presented as more important than the social, the natural, the temporal, and the incidental. But the scream hangs in a social world that is balanced between screams of horror and exclamations of delight.

One place the story returns to time and again is Nate, the blacksmith's shop. 'Oh, beautiful sounds from the blacksmith's shop at the end of the garden!' Small cries, like a series of soft 'Oh's run through the piece. Outside there is, 'the world of sad brown perfume, and morning'. She is in the pasture, thinking of not going home, when as Bishop says: 'But an immense, sibilant, glistening loneliness suddenly faces me, and the cows are moving off.'[34]

But it is Nate at his anvil that keep calling her back. Its *clang, clang* 'turns everything else to silence'[35]. It is a man working. Even the river falls silent but for a once-in-a-while unexpected gurgle. A *Slp* as Bishop writes it.

'Now there is no scream,' she says. 'Once there was one and

it settled slowly down to earth one hot summer afternoon.'[36] Perhaps it has gone away for ever. The story ends:

> It sounds like a bell buoy out at sea.
> It is the elements speaking: earth, air, fire, water.
> All those other things – clothes, crumbling postcards, broken china: things damaged and lost, sickened or destroyed; even the frail almost-lost scream – are they too frail for us to hear their voices long, too mortal?
> Nate!
> Oh, beautiful sound, strike again![37]

Flowing and flown. Those lost clothes, crumbling postcards, and bits of broken china are what animate W.G. Sebald's *Austerlitz*. They are the strange, sad, marvellous intersections of history being remade through human work, through the clangour of the blacksmith's hammer. The world is both communal and solitary, and surely that is the oldest of paradoxes.

There is in these things, in Brodsky's Cape Cod, in Mahon's shed, in W.G. Sebald's vast hotels and burning squares, and in Bishop's village and fishhouses a sense of history as trace, as a sibilant, glistening loneliness that is not so much out there with the machine declaring: *Game Over*, but something soaked into the skin, inscribed in the bones: a sense of human solidarity if you like but without all the consolations of community. The scream is in the bones. The hammer echoes with the icy black sea. Cold dark deep and absolutely clear.

Oh, beautiful sound, strike again!

NOTES

FIRST LECTURE
Cold dark deep and absolutely clear

1. Elizabeth Bishop, *The Complete Poems: 1927-1979* (New York: Farrar, Straus & Giroux, 1986), p. 64; *Complete Poems*, hereinafter CP; 'At the Fishhouses', *CP:ATF*.

2. *CP:ATF*, l. 1-5

3. T.S. Eliot, *The Complete Poems and Plays of T.S. Eliot* (London: Faber & Faber, 1982), 'The Fire Sermon', p. 68.

4. *CP:ATF*, l. 7.

5. ibid, l. 9-11.

6. ibid, l. 29-30.

7. ibid, l. 47-49.

8. ibid, l. 60-61.

9. ibid, l. 67-68.

10. ibid, l. 71-75.

11. Transcript of interview with Dr Sanjay Gupta of CNN. http://transcripts.cnn.com/TRANSCRIPTS/0405/08/hcsg.00.html.

12. *CP:ATF*, l. 76-77.

13. ibid, l. 78-83.

14. 'Dover Beach', l. 16-18, Matthew Arnold, *Poetical Works* (London & Glasgow: Collins), p. 355.

15. ibid, l. 24-28.

16. http://www.english.uiuc.edu/maps/poets/a_f/bishop/fishhouses.htm

17. Sándor Márai, *The Rebels* (New York: Knopf, 2007), pp. 157-58.

18. Claudio Magris, *Danube* (London: Collins Harvill, 1989), p. 19.

19. ibid, p.29.

20. George Szirtes, *Reel* (Tarset: Bloodaxe Books, 2004), p. 91; New & Collected Poems (Tarset: Bloodaxe Books, 2008), p. 436.

21. *CP*, p. 14.

22. *CP*, p. 127.

23. *CP*, p. 159.

24. ibid, l. 15-31.

25. ibid, l. 54-59.

26. ibid l. 90-93.

27. 'Lullaby of Cape Cod', Joseph Brodsky, *A Part of Speech* (Oxford: Oxford University Press, 1980), p. 107.

28. 'Lagoon', *A Part of Speech*, p. 74.

29. 'A Part of Speech', *A Part of Speech*, p. 92.

30. ibid, p.92 l. 1-6.

31. ibid, p.93, l. 3-4 .

32. ibid, p. 93, l. 5-7.

33. See note 27.

34. ibid, part 1, l. 8-10.

35. T.S. Eliot, 'The Love Song of J. Alfred Prufrock', *The Complete Poems and Plays* (London: Faber & Faber, 1969), p. 15.

36. 'A Part of Speech', part I, l. 21.

37. ibid, part II, l. 10-12.

38. ibid, Part III, l. 37-40.

39. ibid, Part VI, l. 14-19.

40. ibid, Part VIII, pp. 2-5.

41. ibid, Part VIII, p. 22-29.

42. See note 28.

43. ibid, l. 7-8.

44. ibid, l. 19-27.

45. ibid, l. 43-48.

46. ibid, l. 49-53.

SECOND LECTURE
Life is Elsewhere

1. Adrian Mitchell, *Poems* (London: Jonathan Cape, 1964), p.viii.

2. Adrian Mitchell, 'Invocation', *Heart on the Left: Poems 1953-1984* (Newcastle upon Tyne: Bloodaxe Books, 1997), p. 42.

3. Adrian Mitchell, 'Loose Leaf Poem', *Heart on the Left*, p. 63.

4. *The Faber Book of Political Verse*, ed. Tom Paulin (London: Faber & Faber, 1986). Hereafter *FBPV*.

5. Paulin 'Introduction' *FBPV*, p. 50.

6. ibid p. 49.

7. ibid, p. 27.

8. ibid, p. 19.

9. ibid p. 18.

10. 'Grass, alas', Martin Bell, *Complete Poems*, ed. Peter Porter (Newcastle upon Tyne: Bloodaxe Books, 1988), p. 88.

11. Paulin, 'Introduction' *FBPV*, p. 16.

12. ibid, p. 18.

13. ibid, p. 17.

14. ibid, p. 51.

15. ibid, p. 52.

16. ibid, p. 52.

17. ibid, p. 52.

18. Milan Kundera, *Life is Elsewhere* (London: Faber and Faber, 1986).

19. Kundera, 'Postscript', *Life is Elsewhere*, p. 309.

20. ibid, p. 309.

21. ibid, p. 310.

22. ibid, p. 310.

23. See 13, above.

24. Zbigniew Herbert, 'Elegy of Fortinbras', *Zbigniew Herbert: Selected Poems* (Harmondsworth: Penguin Books, 1968) p. 98.

25. George Szirtes, Kraców paper, not yet published.

26. *The Penguin Book of Socialist Verse*, ed. Alan Bold (Harmondsworth: Penguin Books, 1970), hereafter *PBSV*.

27. Bold, 'Introduction' PBSV, p.56.

28. *Post-War Polish Poetry*, ed. & tr. Czesław Miłosz (Harmondsworth: Penguin Books, 1970).

29. *Post-War Polish Poetry*, p. 97.

30. Szirtes, Kraców.

31. A. Alvarez, 'Introduction', *Zbigniew Herbert: Selected Poems*, p. 10.

32. Szirtes, Kraców.

33. Gábor Garai, 'A man is beaten up', *PBSV*, p. 452.

34. ibid, l. 20-22.

35. ibid, l. 23-30.

36. ibid, l. 36-39.

37. Gyula Illyés, *Puszták népe* (Budapest: Nyugat, 1936), in English as *People of the Puszta* (Budapest: Corvina, 1967).

38. Gyula Illyés, 'A Sentence about Tyranny', *The Colonnade of Teeth: Modern Hungarian Poetry*, ed. George Gömöri & George Szirtes (Newcastle upon Tyne: Bloodaxe Books, 1996), pp. 31-36.

39. György Petri, *Körülírt zuhanás* (Budapest: Szépirodalmi kiadó, 1973).

40. Clive Wilmer, 'Introduction', *Night Song of the Personal Shadow* (Newcastle upon Tyne: Bloodaxe Books, 1991), p. 10.

41. ibid, p. 12.

42. György Petri, *Eternal Monday: New & Selected Poems* (Newcastle upon Tyne: Bloodaxe Books, 1999), p. 63.

43. ibid, p. 32

THIRD LECTURE
Flowing and flown

1. Derek Mahon, *Collected Poems* (Oldcastle: Gallery Press, 1999), p. 64. Hereafter MCP.

2. 'A Disused Shed in Co. Wexford', *MCP*, p. 65.

3. George Seferis, 'From *Mythical Story*', *Four Greek Poets* (Harmondsworth: Penguin Books, 1970), p. 43.

4. ibid, p. 54.

5. Derek Mahon 'A Disused Shed in Co. Wexford', *MCP*, l. 50-52.

6. ibid, l. 54-59.

7. Derek Mahon, 'The Snow Party', *MCP*, p. 63.

8. All in *MCP*.

9. Derek Mahon, *The Hudson Letter* (Oldcastle: Gallery Press, 1995), pp. 19, 41.

10. *MCP*, p. 124.

11. Brendan Kennelly: 'Derek Mahon's Humane Perspective', *Journey into Joy: Selected Prose*, ed. Åke Persson (Newcastle upon Tyne: Bloodaxe Books, 1994), pp.131-35 (135).

12. William Empson, *Collected Poems* (London: Chatto & Windus, 1977), p. 60.

13. Zsuzsa Rakovszky, *New Life* (Oxford: Oxford University Press, 1994), p. 1.

14. Zsuzsa Rakovszky, *Fehér-fekete* (Pécs: Jelenkor, 1991).

15. *New Life*, pp. 51-53.

16. György Petri, 'A Recognition', *Eternal Monday: New & Selected Poems* (Newcastle upon Tyne: Bloodaxe Books, 1999). p. 90.

17. Ottó Orbán, *The Blood of the Walsungs: Selected Poems* (Newcastle upon Tyne: Bloodaxe Books, 1993) p. 92.

18. Daniela Crasnaru, *Letters from Darkness* (Oxford: Oxford University Press, 1991).

19. Fleur Adcock, 'Foreword', *Letters from Darkness*, p. vii (unnumbered).

20. Tom Paulin, 'Where Art is a Midwife', *The Strange Museum* (London: Faber & Faber), p. 35.

21. Adcock, 'Foreword', p.vii (unnumbered).

22. ibid.

23. ibid.

24. Crasnaru, *Letters from Darkness*, p. 8.

25. ibid, p40.

26. Virág Erdős, 'Vision (Game Over)' in *An Island of Sound: Hungarian Poetry and Fiction before and beyond the Iron Curtain*, ed. Miklós Vajda and George Szirtes (London: The Harvill Press, 2004), pp. 412-13. *Note:* My translation in the lecture is adapted from the version in the book. It is a case of still trying to get it quite right.

27. Elizabeth Bishop, 'In the Village', *The Collected Prose*, ed. Robert Giroux (New York: Farrar, Straus & Giroux; London: Chatto & Windus, 1984), pp. 251-74; hereafter *Collected Prose*.

28. Anne Stevenson, *Between the Iceberg and the Ship: Selected Essays* (Ann Arbor: University of Michigan Press, 1998).

29. ibid, p. 58.

30. *Collected Prose*, p. 251.

31. ibid, p. 254.

32. ibid, p. 257.

33. ibid, p. 261.

34. ibid, p. 265.

35. ibid, p. 274.

36. ibid, p. 274.

37. ibid, p. 274.

George Szirtes was born in Budapest in 1948, arrived in England as a refugee in 1956 and was brought up in London. He was trained as a painter in Leeds and at Goldsmiths College. He has taught art, history of art and creative writing in various schools and colleges, and now teaches poetry and creative writing at the University of East Anglia. For some years he exhibited and ran a small etching and poetry press together with his wife, artist Clarissa Upchurch. He lives in Wymondham, Norfolk.

His poems began to appear in print in the mid 70s. His first book, *The Slant Door*, was awarded the Geoffrey Faber Prize and since then he has won the Cholmondeley Award and been short-listed for the Whitbread and Forward Poetry Prizes. He was elected a Fellow of the Royal Society of Literature in 1982.

After his first return to Hungary in 1984 he translated poetry, fiction and plays from the Hungarian and for his work in this field he has won the European Poetry Translation Prize, the Dery Prize and been shortlisted for the Weidenfeld and Aristeion Prizes as well as receiving the Golden Star medal of the Hungarian republic. He co-edited Bloodaxe's *The Colonnade of Teeth: Modern Hungarian Poetry* (1996) with George Gömöri, and his Bloodaxe edition of Ágnes Nemes Nagy's poetry, *The Night of Akhenaton: Selected Poems* (2004), was a Poetry Book Society Recommended Translation. His study of the artist Ana Maria Pacheco, *Exercise of Power*, was published by Ashgate in 2001. He co-edited the anthology *An Island of Sound: Hungarian Poetry and Fiction before and beyond the Iron Curtain* (Harvill, 2004). He has also written for children, and for various composers in collaboration.

After four collections with Secker and five with Oxford University Press, he moved to Bloodaxe, publishing his Hungarian selection *The Budapest File* in 2000, *An English Apocalypse* in 2001, and *Reel*, winner of the T.S. Eliot Prize, in 2004. *Budapest: Image, Film, Poem*, a collaboration with Clarissa Upchurch, was published by Corvina in 2006. His *New & Collected Poems* was published by Bloodaxe Books in 2008 at the same time as the first full-length collection critical study of his work, *Reading George Szirtes* by John Sears. His latest full-length collection, *The Burning of the Books and other poems* (Bloodaxe Books, 2009), a Poetry Book Society Recommendation, was shortlisted for the T.S. Eliot Prize. He reads a selection of his work on the CD *George Szirtes Reading from his poems* (The Poetry Archive, 2005).